T0271564

Specific Learning Differences –
What Teachers Need to Know

from the same author

Exploring Science with Dyslexic Children and Teens
Creative, Multi-Sensory Ideas, Games and Activities to Support Learning
Diana Hudson
ISBN 978 1 78775 386 0
eISBN 978 1 78775 387 7

of related interest

Learning From Autistic Teachers
How to Be a Neurodiversity-Inclusive School
Edited by Francesca Happé, Rebecca Wood, Dr Laura
Crane, Alan Morrison and Ruth Moyse
ISBN 978 1 83997 126 6
eISBN 978 1 83997 127 3

The British Dyslexia Association – Teaching Dyslexic Students
Theory and Practice
Foreword by Helen Ross
ISBN 978 1 78775 745 5
eISBN 978 1 78775 746 2

The Neurodiverse Classroom
A Teacher's Guide to Individual Learning Needs and How to Meet Them
Victoria Honeybourne
ISBN 978 1 78592 362 3
eISBN 978 1 78450 703 9

Specific Learning Differences – What Teachers Need to Know

Embracing Neurodiversity in the Classroom

SECOND EDITION

DIANA HUDSON

Illustrated by Jon English

Jessica Kingsley Publishers
London and Philadelphia

First published in Great Britain in 2024 by Jessica Kingsley Publishers
An imprint of John Murray Press

2

Copyright © Diana Hudson 2024
Copyright © PDA Society

The right of Diana Hudson to be identified as the Author of the Work has been
asserted by her accordance with the Copyright, Designs and Patents Act 1988.

All rights reserved. No part of this publication may be reproduced, stored in a retrieval system,
or transmitted, in any form or by any means without the prior written permission of the
publisher, nor be otherwise circulated in any form of binding or cover other than that in which
it is published and without a similar condition being imposed on the subsequent purchaser.

All pages marked with ⬇ can be photocopied and downloaded for
personal use with this program, but may not be reproduced for any
other purposes without the permission of the publisher.

A CIP catalogue record for this title is available from the
British Library and the Library of Congress

ISBN 978 1 83997 708 4
eISBN 978 1 83997 709 1

Printed and bound by CPI Group (UK) Ltd, Croydon, CR0 4YY

Jessica Kingsley Publishers' policy is to use papers that are natural, renewable and recyclable
products and made from wood grown in sustainable forests. The logging and manufacturing
processes are expected to conform to the environmental regulations of the country of origin.

Jessica Kingsley Publishers
Carmelite House
50 Victoria Embankment
London EC4Y 0DZ

www.jkp.com

John Murray Press
Part of Hodder & Stoughton Ltd
An Hachette Company

Contents

Acknowledgements

I would like to repeat my thanks to everyone who helped me put together the first edition of this book. Their help was invaluable and has formed the foundations for this second edition.

For this edition my continuing thanks are due to:

- Jon English, the artist, for his wonderful designs for both editions; they bring humour and life to the book
- Meg Scullion for casting her careful eye over the new sections and improving the flow and English.

The following people and organisations have been especially helpful with advising me about new material and resources for neurodiverse students of today. Thank you very much for your support.

- Sue Flohr, manager Adult Dyslexia Centre, member of the European Dyslexia Association
- Amita Jassi, consultant clinical psychologist, Specialist OCD, BDD and Related Disorders Clinic South London and Maudsley NHS Foundation Trust
- Amanda Keen, dyscalculia tutor and accessor
- Marian Mulcahy, senior lecturer UCL Institute of Education, London

- Emma McNally, chief executive and Lucy Toghill, education manager of Tourettes Action
- Ione Georgakis, CAMHS occupational therapist and lead advocate for Tourettes Action
- Jessica Hudson, paediatric doctor specialising in childhood development and neurodisability
- P.J. Balderstone, Scanningpens.com
- Malcolm Little, dyslexia consultant
- Ryan Graham, chief technology officer, Texthelp.

My thanks also go to the following organisations:

- Ambitious about Autism
- British Dyslexia Association
- Dyspraxia Foundation
- Dyscalculia Network
- National Autistic Society
- PDA Society
- Tourettes Action.

Thank you to Amy Lankester-Owen, Laura Savage and the staff at Jessica Kingsley Publishers for their support throughout the production of this book.

My love and special thanks go to my husband Mike for standing by me throughout this project and quietly reminding me to focus and get on with it, and to our children Jenny, Tim, Jessica and Kay for cheerfully backing me and encouraging me to keep my sense of humour; love to you all.

Introduction to the Second Edition

A great deal has changed in the recognition and appreciation of people with different thinking styles since the publication of the first edition of *Specific Learning Difficulties What Teachers Need to Know* in 2015.

It is now generally accepted that there is a range of thinking styles within any population or classroom. This is called neurodiversity. All people have recognised strengths and weaknesses. Outside the extremes of the 'normal spread' of thinking there are individuals who are referred to as being neurodivergent. They often have great talents and skills and can become very successful, but their differences in thinking and learning style may make study at school very challenging. Parents and teachers who are sensitive to the strengths and needs of these students can make a huge difference to their happiness, self-esteem and eventual success.

Being neurodivergent is now more positively accepted in society, and there is a greater tendency to appreciate the talents and skills of people who think differently. Employers are realising that it is an advantage to have a range of thinking styles and will now often actively recruit neurodivergent employees. It is for this reasons that the term 'Specific Learning Difficulties' used in the original book title, has been replaced with 'Specific Learning Differences' in this second edition. For simplicity I will, however, continue to use SpLDs as the shortened version.

Despite greater acceptance, it would be unrealistic to pretend that students who think differently will not face learning or emotional challenges at school. However, supportive, informed and upbeat teachers can make a huge difference to their self-esteem, academic success and future prospects. I hope that this book will help.

The essence of this second edition remains the same as the first. It is to support busy classroom teachers in secondary schools, to provide a better understanding of neurodivergent students and to suggest classroom strategies to support their students who think and learn in different ways.

I ask a series of questions when looking at each identifiable difference.

- What is different about the way that these students think?
- What are their strengths?
- What might they find challenging?
- What can we do as teachers to provide support?

The term Specific Learning Differences normally only includes dyslexia, dyscalculia, dysgraphia and sometimes dyspraxia, but I have broadened the scope of the term for this book. I have included some other differences that affect brain function, learning style and behaviour in the classroom. I have, therefore included attention deficit hyperactive disorder (ADHD), autism spectrum disorder (ASD) and obsessive compulsive disorder (OCD). These may occur concurrently with the conventional SpLDs and some of the challenges these students may experience are shared with others with Specific Learning Differences so I feel that they rightly deserve their place.

This edition also includes three new chapters on:

- Pathological demand avoidance (PDA), which is a trait that is now recognised in a number of autistic children.
- Sensory processing disorder (SPD) which can occur concurrently in people with a range of SpLDs outlined in the book.

- Tics and Tourette syndrome as this often co-occurs with other SpLDs and affects learning and concentration.

The format is as follows:

- Chapter 1 considers brain processing and learning and introduces many of the terms that are used later in the book.
- Chapters 2–11 each cover a different specific difference as outlined in the contents page.
- Chapters 12 and 13 consider organisational skills, revision and exams.
- Chapter 14 a final word.

At the end of the book, the appendices include some downloadable check sheets that can be used to help identify whether a student has one or other of the most common SpLDs. These are not designed to give a diagnosis but are merely a set of indicators that could suggest that it may be worth carrying out further testing. All material marked with a ⏬ can be photocopied or downloaded from www.jkp.com/catalogue/book/9781839977084

You will also find a glossary defining and explaining terms used in the book. There are references, lists of useful websites and further reading relating to each chapter.

It is estimated that in a typical class of 30 there will be one or possibly two students who have a learning difference. They occur equally in all types of school and are unaffected by economic background or ethnicity. These students may appear to be intelligent and articulate but underperform in tests, or they may find being in the classroom difficult and present behavioural challenges in class.

This book is not intended to be read from cover to cover but rather as a 'go-to book' to dip into when needed. I hope that you will enjoy using it and it will give you a sense of perspective and show the potential upsides for students with learning differences. It will also give practical classroom strategies to help you support your students to overcome barriers and achieve their best.

Neurodivergent students can be among the most interesting, challenging and exciting young people to teach, and many will have talents and the potential to become highly successful in their chosen career. As teachers, we must try to unlock their potential and act as their launching pad!

I wish you the very best.

CHAPTER 1

Brains That Work a Little Differently

INTRODUCING SPECIFIC LEARNING DIFFERENCES

★ What are Specific Learning Differences?

★ How do we learn best?

★ Different learning styles

★ Active or passive learning?

★ Processing speed

★ Short- and long-term memory

★ Attention span

★ Executive function skills

★ Hearing and vision

★ Value of diagnosis

★ Scaffolding

★ Specialist software

★ Specific Learning Differences: daunting or exciting?

★ Remember, you are not alone

★ Key points

Within any class of students there will be a range of academic ability, personality, strengths and weaknesses. Usually students will perform in a fairly consistent manner across all subjects, but there may be a few who are very good at some things but have surprisingly weaker results in others. It is this disparity, sometimes known as a 'spiky profile', that often identifies people who have Specific Learning Differences or are neurodivergent thinkers. As teachers it is important to understand how these students think in order to support them to learn effectively and thrive.

WHAT ARE SPECIFIC LEARNING DIFFERENCES?

Previously the term 'Specific Learning Difficulties' was used to describe when there was a disparity in achievement between areas of learning. This has been defined as 'a particular difficulty in one area of learning in a child who performs satisfactorily in other areas' (Worthington 2003).

The term 'Specific Learning Differences' is now thought to be more appropriate as there are advantages of thinking differently as well as the downsides.

These differences often run in families and they occur in all racial groups and economic backgrounds.

People don't 'grow out of' thinking differences, but as teachers we can support them to learn to find a range of coping strategies to support them to overcome any barriers to learning that are the consequence of them. They can learn to take in and retain information, have more positive experiences at school, pass exams and become fulfilled adults in their chosen areas of interest.

If sympathetic and adaptable teachers can support these students to find their own strengths and explore their own preferred learning styles and interests, it can make a huge difference and enable neurodivergent students to blossom.

The neurodivergencies which may be found in mainstream classrooms and affect learning are:

- *Dyslexia:* difficulties with reading, writing and spelling
- *Dyscalculia:* difficulties with numbers and arithmetic
- *Dysgraphia:* physical difficulties with handwriting
- *Dyspraxia:* difficulties with movement and coordination
- *Attention deficit hyperactivity disorder (ADHD):* difficulties with concentration
- *Autism spectrum disorders (ASD):* social and communication difficulties
- *Pathological demand avoidance (PDA):* difficulty carrying out perceived demands (a trait shown by some autistic people)
- *Sensory processing disorders (SPD):* either over- or under-sensitivity to certain stimuli
- *Tics and Tourette syndrome:* uncontrollable movements or noises
- *Obsessive compulsive disorder (OCD):* unfounded worries and fears (obsessions) that lead to repetitive behaviour patterns (compulsions).

All these differences vary in severity along a continuum from mild to severe, so no two students will be the same. There is also considerable co-existence among them, and each learner will have their own 'cocktail' of challenges and strengths (see Figure 1.1). For example, some dyslexic students may also be dyscalculic or have ADHD, others will not. And each and every neurodivergent student is an individual with their own personality and profile so it can be hard to generalise. As a rule of thumb, as much as you are able to, let the child lead the way as you figure out what their learning needs are. In this book I have outlined each of the learning differences separately, but you may need to dip into several chapters if a student has a 'mix' of difficulties.

More information can be found in Appendix 1, which shows a summary of the most common symptoms for each learning difference.

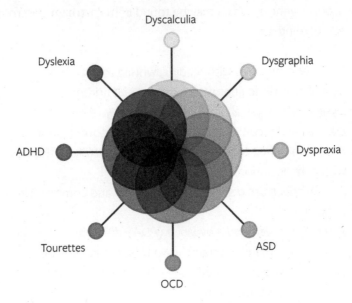

FIGURE 1.1 OVERLAP OF LEARNING DIFFERENCES

It is important to try to understand your students' 'mix' and the extent of their strengths and difficulties so that you can work with them to achieve success.

HOW DO WE LEARN BEST?

We all have strengths and weaknesses and ways that we prefer to learn.

As teachers, we are inclined to teach in the way that we like to learn, so we must continually remind ourselves to try to make adaptations to best suit our students.

We take in information in many ways but primarily:

- what we see
- what we hear
- what we do physically.

The most successful lessons are usually multisensory as the lesson material is reinforced in several different ways making it more memorable.

It is important to remember that some students may have difficulties taking in and remembering material presented in one particular way, and so it is vital to use a variety of approaches to engage with them. Some may also struggle with too much sensory input (see Chapter 9) so techniques may need to be modified.

It is also recognised that some people are sociable with good interpersonal skills, and they will enjoy working in group situations. Others will be more solitary and self-reliant and have strong intrapersonal skills, and they will prefer to work alone.

Sensory input	Teaching methods
Sight	Looking and observing
	Reading text, pictures, diagrams, posters, cartoons, films, charts, displays, handouts, computer graphics, use of colour
Hearing	Listening and speaking
	Stories, songs, audio recordings, question and answer games, making up raps, poems
	Using repetition, rhythm and rhyme
Practical experience	Physical experience
	Craft projects, experimenting, active participation, model making, interactive computer games, board games, acting, role-play

FIGURE 1.2 MULTISENSORY TEACHING IDEAS

It is valuable for teachers to be aware of these preferences for all students but especially for those who are neurodivergent. All students should, however, be encouraged sometimes to work outside their comfort zone, or what is habitual for them, provided this is not unmanageably stressful for them, and this is another advantage of using a multisensory approach.

Above all, try to make your lessons active, stimulating and exciting to keep students engaged.

ACTIVE OR PASSIVE LEARNING?

Active learning is when the students are participating in activities such as group discussions, debating, carrying out experiments, giving presentations or inventing a new teaching resource. The increased learning potential of active learning is clearly demonstrated by the learning graph shown in Figure 1.3.

Students may retain information better if they are actively involved in their own learning process, rather than being passive recipients of information. It is often easy for us as teachers to slip into the 'lecture style' approach, especially when we are racing to 'get through' the syllabus. However, do try to hand over to the students sometimes. You may be amazed by the results.

Also, an opportunity for active learning can be a time when students with different thinking styles have the chance to shine. They can sometimes produce unusual, exciting and stimulating material, which they can show to their peers. This is good for their self-esteem, and we can all enjoy and celebrate their talents.

IDEA

Try getting the students to invent board games or songs linked to a topic. It can be fun.

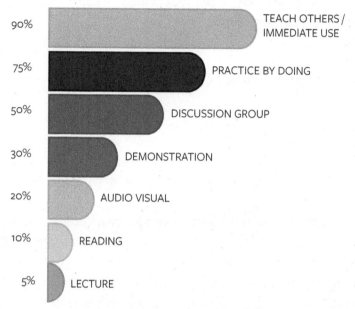

FIGURE 1.3 RETENTION OF INFORMATION
Based on the learning pyramid NTL (National Training Laboratories),
Institute of Applied Behavioral Science in Virginia, USA

PROCESSING SPEED

When we take in information that we see, hear or experience physically it takes a little time to think about it and respond. This is called processing time. The shorter the processing time, the faster thinking and learning can take place.

Some people are described as having a slow processing speed and so they will take longer to absorb the information and think about a response. This does not reflect their overall intelligence or physical issues with sight or hearing. It is just that the interpretation of the information takes longer.

Students with slow processing speed will, therefore, benefit from having a few moments to think prior to answering verbal questions. They can get flustered and be unable to retrieve answers fast enough if asked a sudden question and 'put on the spot'. They will also need longer for processing time in written tests.

SHORT-TERM MEMORY (WORKING MEMORY)

Information that is needed only temporarily, such as a shopping list, a set of instructions or the score in tennis, goes into our short-term memory. This 'working' memory is also essential in order not to get 'lost' when carrying out step-by-step procedures such as mathematical calculations.

If a student has a poor short-term memory they will continually forget instructions, meetings, page numbers, equipment, homework, to name but a few. All information must, therefore, be written or recorded before it is forgotten. Students with short-term memory difficulties will be unable to revise at the last minute for tests or exams. They will have to commit information to their long-term memory in order to fix it. This will likely take longer and need greater repetition and reinforcement.

LONG-TERM MEMORY

We build up and retain a bank of knowledge that can be retrieved for many years, owing to our long-term memories. Once material has been committed to long-term memory, it is much more rooted and may even stay with us for life. Even as adults most of us can remember nursery rhymes or expressions that our parents said to us in childhood.

We are often better able to remember information if we can make some mental connection, such as a rhyme, mnemonic, musical rhythm or funny saying. This makes it more likely to enter the long-term memory.

> Ask any doctor and they are likely to be able to recall at least one dubious rhyme for remembering the names of the cranial nerves.

ATTENTION SPAN

The length of time for which students at secondary school can concentrate on a single activity will vary, but it is a relatively short time, usually around 15 minutes for teenagers.

It is therefore beneficial to change activity several times within a lesson. Some students, including those with ADHD, may have even shorter concentration spans than usual for their age group, and this can affect their ability to learn new material and to perform well. These students can easily become bored and either just 'switch off' or disrupt lessons.

Changing the learning style and pace of the lesson regularly can help to keep students focused. Aim to make progress in short sprints rather than going for a marathon!

EXECUTIVE FUNCTION SKILLS

These skills are related to planning and organising, setting targets, learning from experience and controlling impulsive behaviour. Most teenagers have problems in these areas but gradually improve as they move through secondary school. However, many neurodivergent students have greater difficulty than their peers with organisation and planning. They will probably continue to need support in these areas throughout school.

HEARING

Conditions such as glue ear in young children reduce their hearing accuracy. Even if this physical problem has been remedied, children may have missed an early stage of development when they would have identified sounds made by letters and combinations of letters (phonemes) within words. This can contribute to spelling and reading problems later as they may have not heard words accurately in the past. They commonly miss out syllables when they write, or muddle consonants such as p for b. Some dyslexic children have a history of glue ear in early childhood.

VISION

Some students may have difficulties with tracking, which is the ability to coordinate the two eyes to follow words on a line of print. This can cause great difficulty with reading as they may jump lines or miss out words.

Visual stress is another situation where the eyes do not work correctly together, and this can cause the letters to merge or the lines to jump (see Figure 1.4). Clearly this makes it very difficult to read accurately and to copy from a board. Visual stress and tracking problems can be improved with regular eye exercises, and in some cases it has also been found that changing the colour of the background paper or computer screen can help.

There is not always a link between visual stress and dyslexia but it is often worth investigating as many dyslexic people have eye-tracking difficulties.

If there is any possibility of visual problems causing a student to copy inaccurately or complain of tired eyes and headaches, it is worth asking a specialist behavioural optometrist to investigate further so that the student can receive the correct support

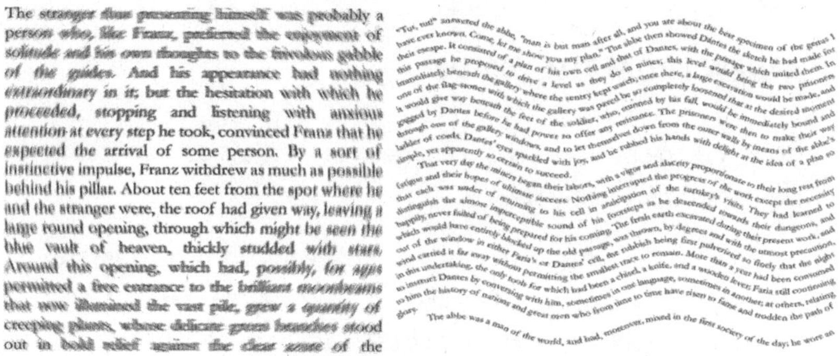

FIGURE 1.4 TWO VIEWS OF VISUAL STRESS
Courtesy of Blackstone Optometrists

VALUE OF DIAGNOSIS

In my experience many students feel a sense of relief when they are given a diagnosis of a neurodivergence. It gives an understanding of any difference and recognises their strengths. It can also be helpful to teachers and parents as specialist reports often give greater insight and advice.

SCAFFOLDING – PROVIDING SUPPORTED LEARNING

Whatever a student's learning difference is they will benefit from continued tailored support from their teachers to gradually build up independence and confidence. The term 'scaffolding' has been adopted recently to describe this approach.

USING SPECIALIST SOFTWARE FOR ASSISTIVE TECHNOLOGY

There is now a great range of assistive technology available, and this can be a huge benefit to students with a variety of learning differences.

A VIEW FROM THE INSIDE

Using text-to-speech software has been the single most important coping strategy in my life.

Thanks to Neil Cottrell who was an intelligent student with severe dyslexia. He gained a first class honours degree in psychology and was founder of the assistive software company LexAble Ltd

The field is changing and developing very rapidly so it is worth seeking up-to-date advice. A list of useful websites and products can be found in the website list relating to this chapter.

Some useful software includes:

- *Voice recognition software:* this can be brilliant for students with severe dyslexia as the software responds to the spoken word and will convert it into written text.
- *Text-to-speech software:* this reads text out loud and can be used with electronic text websites, emails, articles and scanned pages from books.
- *Scanners:* these convert pages into electronic format so that text-to-speech software can then be used. There are now scanners for books so that the text at the centre of the spine is not distorted.
- *Scanning pens:* these are easily transportable and can read out certain words or sentences as needed. They also have dictionary thesaurus and translation facilities. However, special 'exam pens' are available without additional functions.
- *Spell-checking programs:* these have been around for a while but were very poor at interpreting what dyslexic spellers were trying to say. More recently, dyslexic-friendly checkers have been developed which work in a more phonetic and context-based way. These can allow the student to concentrate on content rather than spelling.

All these devices can now be used in exams if they are set in exam mode.

SPECIFIC LEARNING DIFFERENCES: DAUNTING OR EXCITING?

It is exciting and invigorating to be able to support neurodivergent students, to celebrate their strengths, embrace their successes and work with them to conquer areas of learning that they find difficult.

It is more helpful to think in terms of students having learning differences rather than difficulties or disabilities, as they also have many strengths and talents.

A VIEW FROM THE INSIDE

Everyone's brain works differently. Why aren't people celebrated for their contributions and not constantly put down for what they find difficult?

John, a young adult with dyspraxia

I can't emphasise enough how much an understanding and supportive teacher can brighten the outlook and raise the aspirations of students with learning differences. You won't be right all the time, but if the students know that you have faith in them and want them to succeed, that is great for their self-esteem and will support them a long way down the road to their success and fulfilment as adults.

The key is to remain cheerful and upbeat and to ask the students about what helps them the most, as they are the experts on how their thinking works! Be flexible in your approach and don't be afraid to try out different ideas. Sometimes the most whacky ones work the best!

REMEMBER, YOU ARE NOT ALONE

There are other professionals in school who support students with SpLDs and advise their teachers, so do not feel that you are alone. Most schools and colleges have a *SENCO* (special educational needs coordinator) whose job it is to make sure that students' individual needs are catered for by the school. There may also be a *head of pastoral care*, a year head or the *student's tutor* who you can approach with any concerns. Students may attend individual lessons with a *specialist learning support teacher* or see a *doctor* or *physiotherapist* regularly. You may also be able to have a *teaching assistant (TA)* working with you in the classroom if the student needs more support. Make sure that you discuss any worries with the appropriate person and work as a united team.

REFERRING TO NEURODIVERGENT STUDENTS

There has been much debate recently among medical professionals and support organisations about how to refer to people who have learning differences or other specific differences which may attract a formal medical diagnosis. Some more medically orientated organisations advise talking about 'a person who has a condition' (e.g. 'a student who has dyslexia' or 'a student with dyscalculia'). This distances the person from their difference.

However, many neurodivergent individuals as well as the National Autistic Society advise that autism is part of someone's personality and not a 'tag-on' addition so the term should be 'autistic child' or 'PDAer child' rather than a 'child with autism' or 'child with PDA'.

I have therefore changed my terminology in this edition when referring to both autistic and dyslexic students to try to reflect the thinking of today, and have used person-first and identity-first language interchangeably for other identities.

People vary greatly in their sensitivity, however, and my best recommendation would be to ask students (or their parents if they are very young) how they would prefer to be described.

KEY POINTS

- -

- We all have different strengths, weaknesses and preferred ways of learning.
- We take in information through our eyes, ears and physical experiences.
- Some neurodivergent students find it hard to take in and process information that is presented in one way, but they can access it via a different route.
- Lessons are most effective if they are multisensory and involve students in active participation.
- Students may have difficulties with concentration span, processing speeds, working memory and organisation.
- Having learning differences does not affect the overall intelligence of the student.
- A cheerful, proactive and sympathetic teacher can make all the difference.

- -

CHAPTER 2

Dyslexia

★ What is dyslexia?

★ How is dyslexia diagnosed?

★ How can I spot a dyslexic student?

★ Common strengths

★ Common indicators (downsides)

★ Overall approach

★ Classroom strategies

★ Individual support

★ Key points

WHAT IS DYSLEXIA?

Dyslexic people have *difficulty with the written language*, that is with:

- reading
- writing
- spelling.

Dyslexia has been defined as a 'learning difficulty that primarily affects the skills involved in accurate and fluent word reading and spelling' (Rose 2009).

Dyslexia occurs across the full range of intellectual abilities. It is thought to affect up to 10 per cent of the population, with a severity varying along a continuum from mild to severe (British Dyslexia Association n.d.). It can affect both boys and girls.

The term 'developmental dyslexia' is sometimes used; this means that the person is born with this difference and that it has not occurred as a result of an illness or accident. It cannot be cured but coping strategies can be learned.

WHERE DOES THE NAME COME FROM?

Dys comes from the Greek word meaning *difficulty*, and *lexis* comes from the Greek word meaning *word*. So dyslexia means *difficulty with words*.

Dyslexia often runs in families, which suggests that there might be a genetic link.

Brain-imaging techniques show that dyslexic people process information differently from others. They tend to think more in pictures than in words and make rapid lateral connections (Schnep 2014). This can be very advantageous in some circumstances and walks of life.

Hearing problems in early childhood, such as glue ear, or visual weakness such as eye-tracking difficulties, do not themselves cause dyslexia but they can be contributory factors (see Chapter 1).

HOW IS DYSLEXIA DIAGNOSED?

Dyslexia is diagnosed by a suitably qualified specialist teacher or an educational psychologist. A thorough diagnostic test is carried out.

HOW CAN I SPOT A DYSLEXIC STUDENT?

Dyslexia is often discovered because of a discrepancy between a student's good oral ability and their mediocre to poor performance on paper.

Look out for a student who makes sensible and intelligent contributions in class but consistently comes out with written test and exam results which are lower than expected, despite hard work. They might also appear to make 'careless' mistakes due to misreading questions or instructions.

COMMON STRENGTHS

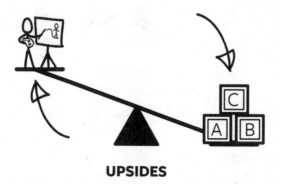

UPSIDES

- Innovative and imaginative thinker.
- Good visualisation and spatial skills.
- Thinks very rapidly in pictures.
- Makes lateral connections in thinking.
- Often creative: good sense of colour and texture, may excel at art, design and photography.
- May be good verbally.
- Can be very quick witted.
- May be good at the performing arts or debating.
- Holistic, sees the whole picture.
- Can multi-task.
- Intuitive problem solver.

- Often hard working and tenacious.
- High emotional intelligence, empathetic.
- Good interpersonal skills.
- Valuable and supportive team member.
- Entrepreneurial.

COMMON INDICATORS (DOWNSIDES)

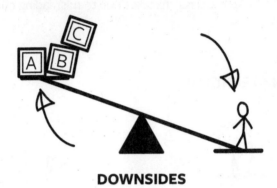

DOWNSIDES

Dyslexic students will show some of the indicators listed below, but probably not all of them, so it can be confusing. Remember also that this can be further complicated as some students may have other Specific Learning Differences as well as dyslexia. And everyone is an individual, so no two dyslexic students will have exactly the same strengths and difficulties profile.

Reading

- Slow reading speed.
- Reading is often inaccurate.
- May not always understand what they have read as they are concentrating on deciphering the words, so may miss the overall meaning.
- Reading inaccuracies may increase under pressure. Liable to make more mistakes in tests.
- May often substitute a similar looking word often starting with

and ending with the same letter. For example, 'silky pyjamas' could become 'silly pyjamas'.

- May have difficulty with written comprehension, often due to misreading words, or missing out key words in the text.
- May be daunted by large chunks of texts and small print.
- May well dislike reading out loud as may be hesitant or make mistakes. Worried about being laughed at.

Spelling

- May show inconsistent spelling of the same word, often within a single piece of writing.
- May have difficulty with phonology (hearing the sounds in words). May miss out syllables of words, for example 'diffulty' for 'difficulty'.
- May confuse consonants, for example g and q or b and p.

My daughter called potatoes 'botatoes' for years!

Author

- May use letter reversals, for example writing *brian* for *brain*.
- Can do well in spelling tests of pre-determined words but spelling 'goes to pieces' when writing an account, as concentration is on the content rather than the spelling.
- Names of people and places may often be misspelt and variable.

Writing

- May have slow writing speed.
- May have difficulties with spelling and punctuation.
- May find it difficult to think about the content and spelling at the same time, so if the content is good, the spelling can be poor. Conversely, if the student's concentration flow is

disrupted by thinking about spelling, then the content is likely to be stilted.

- Their written piece may be much shorter and simpler than expected as the student will avoid certain words if they are unsure of the spelling and stick to 'safe' short words.
- Capital letters may be used randomly throughout a piece of writing.
- Writing may be difficult to read as letters such as a, d, g and q may not be fully formed.
- May have difficulty organising thoughts clearly and logically, so essays may veer off on tangents.
- May fail to answer the question, either due to misreading the question itself, failing to understand it or due to drifting away from the topic.

Note-taking

- May not be able to copy accurately from a board. May copy spellings incorrectly, miss out words or jump lines.
- May not keep up with dictation.
- May show inaccuracies in notes taken in class, especially in a foreign language or with chemical symbols.
- May be unable to process and understand information at the same time as writing down notes.

Mathematics

Some dyslexic students may be good at mathematics but make errors when interpreting questions.

- They may misunderstand questions at language level – maths vocabulary is quite extensive and can be confusing.
- They may confuse symbols such as + with × and ÷ with –.
- They may not be able to read instructions effectively.
- Algebra can be especially difficult if letters such as b, d, p, q, are used.

- Short-term memory problems may cause difficulty retaining numbers long enough for the next step of a calculation.
- They may do number reversals so 28 becomes 82.

Some students may also have dyscalculia (see Chapter 3).

Concentration

- Can get distracted easily.
- May have a short concentration span.
- May make rapid lateral mental leaps and connections, so can go widely off topic – 'grasshopper mind'.
- Thoughts may be disconnected and not seem organised or sequential.

Slow processing speed

- May take longer to answer questions either orally or in writing. Sometimes this is due to having to change information mentally into pictures before it can be decoded and worked on.
- May be liable to panic under pressure and mind 'goes blank', even with something they know well.

Poor short-term memory

- May have difficulties remembering instructions – following experiments or recipes, doing homework, handing home work in.
- May have difficulty retaining numbers for calculations.
- May have difficulty remembering what to write down.

Learning information

- May be unable to revise quickly and 'cram' for tests due to a poor short-term memory.

- May take longer to learn as facts have to be committed to long-term memory.
- May struggle to find effective revision techniques.

Tests and exams (see Chapter 13)

- Can underachieve, causing a discrepancy between oral performance and written test performance.
- May not be able to read the question accurately, so may make apparently 'careless' mistakes.
- May have difficulty organising thoughts clearly and logically for long answers and essays.
- May run out of time.
- May panic or become overloaded.

Organisation (see Chapter 12)

- May forget instructions or directions.
- May have a poor sense of direction so can get lost easily.
- May confuse left and right.
- May misread timetables and instructions and have difficulty telling the time.
- May have difficulty reading an analogue clock.
- May get distracted and forget the time.
- May forget to bring equipment, books, notes, homework.
- May lose belongings.
- May confuse names of places and people, especially if they begin with the same letter.

Sensitive, emotional responses

- May feel upset and humiliated in class.
- May take comments to heart. May be upset by negative feedback or criticism.
- May be easily discouraged, leading to low self-esteem.
- May be sensitive and can lack self-confidence.

- Can be daunted by complex tasks.
- Can decide to play the class jester to gain credit among peers and to give an 'excuse' for not doing so well.

Fatigue

Generally a dyslexic student has to put more effort into keeping up with work and this leads to increased tiredness, stress and anxiety.

CASE STUDY: DYSLEXIA

Learning French vocabulary was a nightmare for 12-year-old Jay who had dyslexia. He had enough trouble learning and spelling English words and found it too difficult and boring. His vocabulary book was just a list of words and was very dull.

His mother helped him enormously. They labelled objects around the house and used his favourite possessions where possible. Sometimes they made models together at weekends to illustrate his weekly French word list. When possible, his teacher let his mother have a copy of the vocabulary list in advance so that she could put some ideas together. Making models made learning fun and gave Jay a mental image to underpin the words to. By speaking the words out loud and making up songs or using rhythm they also re-enforced the vocabulary, helping his oral recall. French learning became an enjoyable weekly game and his confidence grew. Spelling was still difficult but he was able to contribute in class and feel a sense of achievement. He was also very pleased to show off his speaking skills on a holiday in Paris.

Takeaway idea: *A multisensory approach to learning dry facts can make a huge difference for dyslexic students. Informed parents can also be enormously supportive.*

OVERALL APPROACH

- Be supportive, approachable and upbeat.
- Use a multisensory approach where possible.
- Remember that dyslexic students may need more time to interpret and answer written questions.
- Work with the student to devise successful learning strategies.
- Keep cheerful and be willing to try new approaches.
- Let it be known that you believe in their ability.

CLASSROOM STRATEGIES

Seating

Make sure that dyslexic students sit near the front. This has several advantages:

- They can see the board clearly, which will aid reading.
- They are more likely to keep engaged with the lesson and not get distracted.
- You can see their work easily and know how they are doing.
- You can check that information and homework instructions are written down correctly.

Reading

- Dyslexic students may take longer to read a text and they may also not be able to process the content at the same time.
- Reading accuracy may be poor so encourage them to read instructions slowly, twice.
- Try printing on different coloured backgrounds. It is worth experimenting. Find out what suits your student.
- Encourage the use of highlighters to emphasise key words in questions.
- Investigate the use of reading rulers to avoid jumping lines (see resources list for this chapter).

- Question papers should be well spaced out and full sized.

Reading out loud

This can very understandably be a major source of panic, stress and embarrassment for some students. They will dread the moment when they are asked to read out loud. You could ask a dyslexic student if they are happy reading aloud in the first place. You should never make it obligatory as they may simply not feel comfortable or safe doing so. If a dyslexic student is happy to read aloud, below are some tips to support them:

- Do not suddenly ask them to read out loud.
- Some students will be happy to read if they have had a chance to see the passage in advance.
- A larger print copy of a text is sometimes easier to read.
- Many dyslexic students are good actors, presenters and orators but have trouble sight reading. Give them the text in advance. (Some very talented dyslexic actors have to learn the audition scripts.)

Spelling

- Create a list of key spellings for each topic.
- Students could make a vocabulary book or glossary.
- Use colour to liven up vocabulary lists, especially in foreign languages. Perhaps nouns could be on one colour paper, verbs on another.
- Mnemonics can be brilliant for difficult spellings. If they are funny they are more memorable. Look up some for your subject or get the students to make some up.
- Use any tricks or jokes you can think of to help fix the spelling of difficult words in your own subject.
- A spell checker is useful for written assignments, but make sure the student is aware that it will not recognise spelling errors if they make another recognisable word. Phrases such as 'The Duck of Wellington' will pass unchanged.

Giving notes in class

Remember, dyslexic students struggle to write and process information at the same time.

- Ideally give out printed notes. Notes with gaps to fill in are often a good compromise. These can be personalised with illustrations or annotations, but the writing process is much less arduous. You also know that the students have the correct material to learn from.
- If you are handwriting on a board make sure your own writing is clear, large and easy to read.
- Dictation: always write up any key words or awkward spellings on the board, don't go too fast. Try to avoid if possible.
- Check their work regularly, as there are likely to be many errors.
- Students with severe dyslexia may benefit from recording the lesson electronically and listening to it again later or by using specialist software, as outlined in Chapter 1.

Making presentations

Make presentations simple, fun, lively and memorable.

- Do not try to put too much information on each slide – one point per slide.
- Use double spacing.
- Use a clear simple font (without a serif) such as Arial, Calibri, Trebuchet.
- Include diagrams or cartoons.
- Vary the background colour and writing. Some combinations are much clearer for dyslexic readers.
- Read the writing out loud to the students and explain further if needed.

Making worksheets (see Figure 2.1)

- Keep sentences short and clear.
- Space information out well: use double spacing.

- Use a large (12 or 14 point) clear font.
- Break up the page with bold headings, subheadings and indentations.
- Use bullet points.
- Add diagrams, cartoons and other visual markers.
- Use colour – although this may be expensive it is excellent if you can use it.
- Print on coloured paper.
- Make the worksheets clear and attractive.

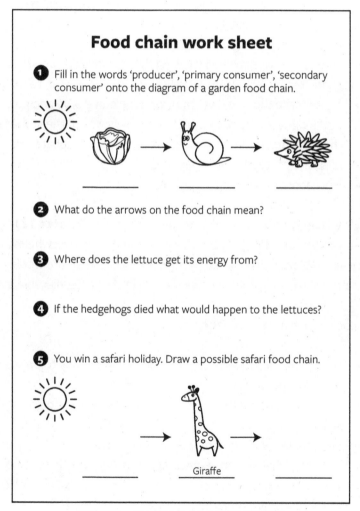

Food chain work sheet

1 Fill in the words 'producer', 'primary consumer', 'secondary consumer' onto the diagram of a garden food chain.

2 What do the arrows on the food chain mean?

3 Where does the lettuce get its energy from?

4 If the hedgehogs died what would happen to the lettuces?

5 You win a safari holiday. Draw a possible safari food chain.

Giraffe

FIGURE 2.1 EXAMPLE OF A WORKSHEET

Studying set texts

Dyslexic people tend to be holistic or 'gist' thinkers and like an idea of the 'big picture' before studying the detail.

- Give an overview of the story at the outset.
- Let students know in advance the text or chapters to read so that they can do so before the lesson.
- Is there a larger print version of the book available?
- Is the book available in an unedited audio version?
- Film versions can be useful to give an overview of the plot and bring the characters to life, but remind students that they may differ from the original text.
- Illustrations or diagrams showing the relationships between the characters can be useful visual resources and are fun to make.
- Try to make the book, poem or passage come alive and go into long-term memory by acting out sections of the stories in the students' own words, dressing up or having debates from different characters' perspectives.
- How about converting a poem to a rap or song?

Essay writing, course work and projects (see Chapter 12)

These can be very daunting as dyslexic students feel overwhelmed by perceived 'big' tasks. They tend to see the magnitude of the whole project rather than being able to break it down into small, achievable goals.

You can provide a lot of support by:

- reminding the students of what they know already to provide a basis for the task and increase confidence
- dividing the task into smaller manageable 'chunks' to give a scaffold for doing the task
- giving dates when different sections are due
- outlining what you are expecting in terms of length/word count
- asking for each section to be handed in so you can check that the students are on target.

Setting homework

- Set homework early in the lesson.
- Keep instructions clear.
- Give guidance about the length of time you expect students to take.
- Remember that it may take a dyslexic student much longer to complete a piece of work, so indicate what is essential and what could be tackled 'if time'.
- Say clearly when homework should be handed in and where to put it.
- Ideally have the homework task written out on a handout, including page numbers and questions. If the students write it down themselves, check for accuracy.
- Can the homework details be recorded electronically? Some schools will let students write or dictate their homework onto a mobile phone.
- Many schools now have an intranet where homework details could be placed.

Enjoyable homework for dyslexic students

Sometimes set imaginative homework tasks which allow dyslexic students to use their talents. Teachers could ask students to:

- draw a series of pictures or cartoons to illustrate the work
- annotate a picture that you provide
- make up a song/poem/rap/advertisement
- plan a debate about an issue
- make up a game, word search, crossword puzzle. (I suggest you check first that the spellings are correct for these!)
- prepare a short dramatic presentation
- record a short voice play or monologue
- make a short film
- make a model.

Marking homework

- Mark for content, not spelling. Remember that there is often a disparity between academic ability and written English as the example below shows:

We wereGiven Helmets. Caves = limestone only cos it is the only rock that can be disolved in water. Fell Beck made the cave, then fawnd a lower passsige. Made a wall of Tufa held back lake. They blowed it up. There was a micro invironment in the cave, where the lite had grew there. Tufa grew on moss. Calsite crystals were glinting

Elefants legs = piller

Copper = Tercoise

Algee = tercoise

Ion = brown

Peet = brown

Thanks to Neil Cottrell founder of LexAble Ltd for permission to use an extract from his geography fieldwork notes, Year 6

- Avoid crossing out every spelling mistake. The correct version could be written in the margin or underneath.
- Do not correct all the language and punctuation errors. Decide what is important in each piece of work.
- Write at the bottom any key words which were misspelt so that they can be written into a glossary and learned.
- Try to write a positive constructive comment such as 'Well done, I especially liked your vivid description.'

- Keep other comments constructive and upbeat, 'Next time think about...'.
- Depending on your school's marking policy, it is sometimes a relief to mark without giving a grade but just a written comment.
- Consider giving two marks, especially for creative projects: one, for academic content and the other, for overall 'artistic' presentation/originality. This is a useful way of acknowledging creativity and original thinking.

Using specialist software

Dyslexic students may benefit greatly from using specialist software as outlined in Chapter 1. Text-to-speech and voice recognition equipment can make a huge difference.

Organisation (see Chapter 12)

Dyslexic people often have very genuine difficulties with organisation. They may misread instructions, get lost, forget equipment and arrive late and exhausted to lessons. Planning ahead and meeting deadlines can also cause difficulty and the student will need guidance.

INDIVIDUAL SUPPORT

An *adult mentor* is a great support for dyslexic students. This can be a teacher, teaching assistant, year head, tutor or a specialist from the learning support department. They key to success is building a relationship and raising the student's self-confidence

This can be aided by:

- **R**egularly meeting with their mentor to iron out difficulties as they arise, boost confidence and celebrate successes
- **R**eminding students what they know already, in order to provide a sound base for new material
- **R**einforcing by revisiting and testing familiar material often

- **R**elaxing and making learning fun using multisensory approaches
- **R**evision: finding effective revision strategies.

Time keeping

Reading an analogue clock can be really difficult for some dyslexic people, so they may genuinely not know the time. A digital watch is a good idea. Alarms can be set on digital watches or phones to remind them when to set off for lessons.

Revision and examinations (See Chapter 13)

Dyslexic students need to develop revision strategies to commit information into their long-term memory. They will also need guidance when sitting exams.

Getting lost

Usually in secondary schools the students move from lesson to lesson. This can be very worrying for a dyslexic student if they have a poor sense of direction.

A plan of the school layout and a timetable with lesson rooms marked will help, provided the student can understand it. Colour coding sometimes helps.

Make sure the students can tell the difference between left and right (see Figure 2.2).

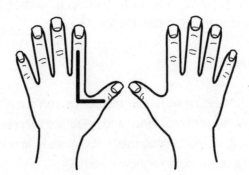

FIGURE 2.2 THE LEFT HAND MAKES THE LETTER L

Outside school, plans of routes or maps are useful in either paper or electronic form. The student will need to factor in time for getting lost until they are familiar with a route, and learn to arrive early or make a practise visit first to be sure of getting to the correct place on time, especially for important appointments. This is something I still do today!

KEY POINTS

- -

- Dyslexia is a problem with reading, writing and spelling.
- It affects about 10 per cent of the population.
- It is not linked to general overall intelligence.
- Organisational skills can also be poor.
- Dyslexic students can learn coping strategies to work around their difficulties.
- Multisensory teaching techniques are important.
- Sensitive classroom teachers can make a huge difference.

- -

CHAPTER 3

Dyscalculia

The aim of this chapter is to help all subject teachers who may have number work, calculations or graphs as part of their syllabus. It is not just confined to teaching the subject of maths.

★ What is dyscalculia?

★ How is dyscalculia diagnosed?

★ How can I spot a student with dyscalculia?

★ Common strengths

★ Common indicators (downsides)

★ Overall approach

★ Classroom strategies

★ Individual support

★ Key points

WHAT IS DYSCALCULIA?

People with dyscalculia have difficulty understanding numbers and therefore struggle with all numerical concepts, including counting, arithmetic, estimating the relative size of numbers and remembering number sequences.

Dyscalculia has been defined as *'a specific and persistent difficulty in understanding numbers which can lead to a diverse range of difficulties with mathematics. It will be unexpected in relation to age, level of education and experience and occurs across all ages and abilities'* (British Dyslexia Association n.d.).

In England, dyscalculia became recognised as a separate Specific Learning Difference (SpLD) in 2004.

WHERE DOES THE NAME COME FROM?

Dys comes from the Greek word meaning difficulty. *Calculia* comes from the Latin word meaning *counting*. So dyscalculia means *difficulty with counting*.

Around 6 per cent of the population have dyscalculia often in combination with another SpLD.

Dyscalculia is found equally in boys and girls. It often runs in families so it is thought to have a genetic component. It cannot be cured but, with effective teaching, students can gain a better understanding of numbers and devise effective coping strategies to succeed in adult life.

HOW IS DYSCALCULIA DIAGNOSED?

There is now a specific assessment test for dyscalculia. This should be carried out by a suitably qualified specialist with relevant training.

HOW CAN I SPOT A STUDENT WITH DYSCALCULIA?

Look out for the student who performs much better verbally and in written assignments, than in tasks where numbers and calculations are involved. They might also be inaccurate with number recall, lack confidence in arithmetic and try to avoid number work wherever possible.

COMMON STRENGTHS

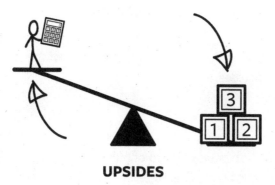

UPSIDES

- Often literate and an expressive writer.
- Poetic and artistic.
- Good problem solvers and lateral thinkers.
- Intuitive.
- Imaginative, artistic and creative, with a good sense of colour and texture.
- Often good memory skills for language-based information.
- Good verbally.
- Empathetic and sensitive to others.
- Outgoing and good at public speaking or acting.
- Resourceful and tenacious.
- Good strategist.

COMMON INDICATORS (DOWNSIDES)

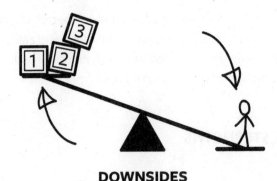

DOWNSIDES

Most students with dyscalculia only show some of the following number-based difficulties.

Numbers

- May lack an intuitive grasp of numbers: may not automatically know which number is larger or smaller than another.
- May be unable to subitise (recognise number patterns) to tell how many items there are in a small group without counting them individually each time. Think of recognising the number of dots on a dice.
- May have trouble rounding numbers up or down.
- May have difficulty estimating answers.
- May often count on fingers.
- May confuse similar looking numbers such as 3 and 8 or 6 and 9.
- May reverse numbers, for example 350 for 305.
- Can have problems with zeros – can be out by multiples of 10.
- May find counting backwards difficult.
- May have extreme difficulty learning times tables as cannot count in sets of numbers, such as 5s.
- Cannot do mental arithmetic.
- May fail to see connections between known number

relationships. For example, if 3 + 5 = 8, then 5 + 3 = 8 or 30 + 50 = 80.

- Can find it difficult to remember mathematical procedures: may have to keep re-learning them.
- If a procedure has been learned it may be followed mechanically and without confidence or understanding.
- May not be sure whether a procedure will make the answer larger or smaller.
- May have difficulty grasping percentages, decimal points and fractions.
- May not be easily able to transfer skills or procedures learned in solving one set of problems to tackle different problems.

Understanding written questions

- Inclined to panic and go blank with number questions, especially when under pressure.
- May have difficulty working out what a question is asking.
- May confuse maths symbols in questions, such as ÷ and −, + and x, < and >.
- May misread or misunderstand the words in questions.
- Can be confused by brackets.
- Liable to guess numerical answers.

Short-term/working memory
Sequencing difficulties cause difficulty remembering:

- numbers to work on during calculations
- a series of processes or instructions
- number sequences, such as phone numbers or security codes
- scores in games or moves when playing strategic games such as chess.

More complex mathematical procedures
Not surprisingly these cause more problems, especially if the basics are shaky. Students may have difficulties with:

- remembering the formulae to solve problems, e.g. area, volume, mass, speed, acceleration
- temperature conversions
- money, especially converting currencies
- percentage increase or decrease
- negative values
- equations, especially if they involve fractions
- statistics, mean, median, mode, standard deviation.

Graphical representation

- May have difficulty understanding and interpreting graphs.
- Knowing which way round the axes should be drawn can be difficult.
- May have difficulty getting the scales to fit the paper.
- Scales may not be consistent or inappropriate.
- Points may not be accurately plotted.
- May make inaccurate readings.

Getting somewhere on time

Telling the time can be a genuine problem. Students may have difficulty reading an analogue or 24-hour clock. As a result, estimating journey times or how long tasks may take can be inaccurate.

Reading and understanding timetables or maps with grid references can also be a problem, so they may get lost easily or arrive late.

Emotional responses

Students with dyscalculia may find themselves embarrassed in class, afraid of being asked a question and shown up in front of their peers. They often panic under pressure and will come up with elaborate, avoidance tactics to bypass maths. Extreme cases can lead to anxiety and 'maths phobia'.

Organisational skills (see Chapter 12)

Some students may have problems with organisation. This is covered separately as it is a common difficulty with several of the SpLDs.

Be alert to dyscalculia – if you suspect that a student has dyscalculia ask the SENCO (special educational needs coordinator) if it is possible to arrange for the student to be professionally tested. This could make a big difference.

A VIEW FROM THE INSIDE

Just because you can't count doesn't mean you don't count.

From It Just Doesn't Add Up *by Professor Paul Moorcraft, author, lecturer and war correspondent with dyscalculia*

CASE STUDY: DYSCALCULIA

Jamila could not get to grips with numbers. Times tables were a problem and she struggled to read a clock. As she moved into secondary school she became more anxious about maths lessons and tried to avoid being asked any questions. Sometimes she avoided maths lessons altogether by pretending to be ill. She spent a much longer time doing maths homework than her peers and began to get stressed and agitated. Despite her intelligence and aptitude for other subjects she ended up in a bottom division for maths and going to special maths coaching.

To her relief her new teacher was kind and non-judgemental and the classroom was a 'safe' zone where mistakes were seen as part of learning. She was introduced to practical aids to represent numbers showing their relationships in a concrete way that she could relate to. Lots of hands-on learning went on both inside the classroom and outside. At last Jasmine could begin to relax and even enjoy some aspects of maths. She discovered that she was especially good at 3D shapes and geometry. She will never have a great aptitude for number work but she is no longer afraid to have a go.

Takeaway idea: *Make number work as practical as possible for students with dyscalculia or maths anxiety. Have fun and make it safe to make mistakes.*

OVERALL APPROACH

- Be sensitive, understanding and supportive.
- Talk to the student about what works well for them. Be willing to try different multisensory approaches or aids to support numeracy.
- Show that you value their intelligence and will work with them to overcome number difficulties.

CLASSROOM STRATEGIES

- Make the classroom a safe, relaxed place where it is OK to make mistakes and to ask questions.
- Do not cause embarrassment.
- Keep students with dyscalculia near the front of the class. This helps engagement and also enables you to keep an eye on their progress.
- Give short, clear instructions.
- Give oral as well as written instructions.
- Make teaching multisensory with practical examples and models.
- Have counting aids available, such as number lines, an abacus or counting rods.
- Repeat any key points.
- Work through an example on the board, slowly and clearly.
- Check regularly that everyone understands.

- Give time for students to write down the example and explain exactly how you would like it to be laid out on the page.
- If you have handed out printed sheets, read them out loud with the class and emphasise key points in a procedure.
- Encourage students to read questions carefully and to take special notice of the symbols and key words.
- Leave enough time to go through the answers in class.
- If a student has 'not got it', try to arrange a quiet time to go through it with them individually, maybe explaining in a different more multisensory way.
- If you want the whole class to work out a quick calculation, mini-white boards can be used and held up for you to see. These are fun and other students will not know who has got the right or wrong answer.
- Do not ask a student with dyscalculia a sudden number question in class.

Mathematical language

- Choose your language carefully. There are many words for the same mathematical processes and these can be confusing (Figure 3.1).
- Be consistent with your words.
- Try to liaise with colleagues in other subjects; it increases confusion if teachers use different words for the same process.

Printed sheets

- Do not put too many examples on a sheet.
- Use a large, simple font.
- Leave white space. Crowded sheets are daunting and small print causes anxiety.
- Make handouts more fun with the odd cartoon.
- Lay examples out clearly. Showing where an answer is to be written.
- Where appropriate, indicate the units to be used.

- Try using other paper colours rather than white. This might be clearer for some students.

ANSWER LARGER	**+**	**X**
> ↑	Plus Add Addition Sum of And How many altogether	Times Multiply Multiplication Sets or groups of product
ANSWER SMALLER	**−**	**÷**
< ↓	Minus Take away Subtract Subtraction Take … from … Difference between How much greater is --- than ---	Divide Division Share Share between How many … in … How many times can … be taken away from … How many times can … go

FIGURE 3.1 COMMON MATHEMATICAL PROCESSES

Counting

Students with dyscalculia are generally unable to estimate numbers quickly from a pattern and so they will have to count laboriously. Be aware that this will take much longer. Lack of confidence may also mean that they may recheck several times.

Fingers are really useful to count with, so let them know that this is fine.

(Many adults with dyscalculia will still count on their fingers under the table due to embarrassment.)

Bigger or smaller?

As students with dyscalculia struggle to understand the relative size of numbers it is a great help to have to have simple number lines available for use (Figure 3.2).

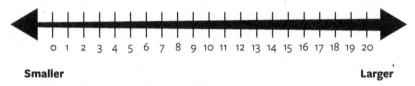

Smaller   **Larger**

FIGURE 3.2 SIMPLE NUMBER LINE

Times tables

Some people with dyscalculia really struggle to learn and remember times tables, especially the more difficult ones such as 7, 8 or 9 times. Even if they are memorised for a test they are likely to be forgotten. It may help to let them have a times table square to refer to (Figure 3.3) These are clearer if different colours are used for each column. Some students find it easier to have a sheet with each times table written separately.

X	1	2	3	4	5	6	7	8	9	10	11	12
1	1	2	3	4	5	6	7	8	9	10	11	12
2	2	4	6	8	10	12	14	16	18	20	22	24
3	3	6	9	12	15	18	21	24	27	30	33	36
4	4	8	12	16	20	24	28	32	36	40	44	48
5	5	10	15	20	25	30	35	40	45	50	55	60
6	6	12	18	24	30	36	42	48	54	60	66	72
7	7	14	21	28	35	42	49	56	63	70	77	84
8	8	16	24	32	40	48	56	64	72	80	88	96
9	9	18	27	36	45	54	63	72	81	90	99	108
10	10	20	30	40	50	60	70	80	90	100	110	120
11	11	22	33	44	55	66	77	88	99	110	121	132
12	12	24	36	48	60	72	84	96	108	120	132	144

FIGURE 3.3 TIMES TABLE SQUARE

If the multiplication itself is not the main theme of your lesson, allow them to use a calculator and do not worry too much. Be aware that however hard they try, many students will still be unlikely to memorise and retain their times tables (Figure 3.4 gives an example of one possible strategy).

A visual way to learn the 9x table

Fold down the finger of the number you want to multiply by

Count the rest of the fingers

The fingers to the left of the folded finger represent tens, and the fingers to the right of the folded finger represent units

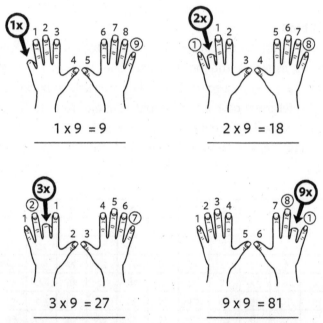

FIGURE 3.4 HANDY WAY TO REMEMBER THE 9 TIMES TABLE

Presentation

Teach students to lay out arithmetic clearly.

- Use paper with ruled squares. Try different sizes.
- Use large sheets of paper.

- Use worksheets with gaps to fill in, and limit the writing required.
- Encourage underlining headings.
- Rule off after each example. This is better if it is in pencil to avoid smudging ink.

Teaching formulae and rules

- If it is important, give students a printed copy.
- Use colour to reinforce learning.
- Drawings may help.
- Use memory aids such as flashcards, mnemonics, song, rap and rhythm.

Multisensory teaching

Try to make examples as multisensory as possible and related to real-life examples.

- Use solid materials that students can see, touch and relate to. Sometimes the crazier the example, the better.
- There are some commercially available colourful and attractive mathematical materials, such as Cuisenaire rods, Numicon, and 3D teaching shapes from listed suppliers.
- Visual aids – posters, models and hands-on discovery. There are several suppliers of posters and models but, if time permits, let students make their own. This is fun, reinforces the learning point and can make an attractive classroom display.
- Use everyday stuff, such as the following:
  - tape measures
  - metre rules
  - rope/string
  - children's building blocks
  - Plasticine or modelling clay
  - plastic bottles
  - boxes, cereal packets
  - coloured beads

- playing cards
- counters.
- Computer programs – some good interactive programs are available.

Here are a just a few kinaesthetic multisensory examples:

- Volume can be demonstrated using different sizes and shapes of boxes, measuring cylinders or kitchen measuring jugs. Sand, grain or dried beans can be used to fill the space and then the volume measured. Coloured water can also be used if the containers are waterproof.

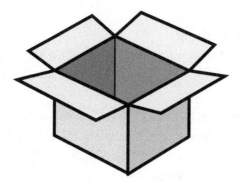

My biology class were intrigued to see the average daily urine output displayed as coloured yellow water in a series of 500ml plastic drinks bottles – much easier to comprehend and remember than a figure in a book!

Author

- Surface area to volume ratios – use potatoes to make chips of the same length and thickness and then cut the chips into different numbers of blocks. This shows the same volume but differing surface areas. Children's bricks can also be used.

- Circles and pie charts – roll out balls of modelling clay into circles and cut out slices. Some cheeses are also circular, with individual sections wrapped. This illustration could be even more memorable if cake is introduced one lesson!

- Percentages – use 100cm³ (100ml) measuring cylinders and coloured water filled to different levels.
- Movement, speed, acceleration – some children's toys can also be fun here, such as wooden toy trains for electric circuits; they can even carry different numbers of currants (pun intended, not a dyslexic error!).
- Balance – use see-saws (from a doll collection, or simply use a ruler balanced on a rubber). Metal coat hangers can be used to make a simple mobile.

Setting homework

- Remember, students with dyscalculia will be slower than their peers, so decide which questions must be done and which should be tackled only if they have time.
- Be clear how much time you expect them to work for. Some students will struggle on for hours. Others will give up and not try.
- Give homework instructions early in the lesson.
- Write the homework on a board, or give out printed instructions and read aloud as well.

- If school allows, students could put the homework into their mobile phone 'notes'.
- Find out if you can put homework on the school intranet.
- Do not set too many examples as this becomes daunting.
- Say exactly when and where homework is to be handed in.

Marking

- Try to mark frequently to make sure that the students are progressing well and understand.
- Be encouraging. If the method is correct but there is a mathematical error or transposed numbers, be positive and just point out where the error is. Try to give marks for method.
- Acknowledge progress, and not only when they get everything right. Stickers or stars are usually popular.

INDIVIDUAL SUPPORT

Students with dyscalculia will benefit from individual specialist teacher support and extra time in examinations. A main part of the individual sessions will be to:

- reinforce lesson material using practical examples and where possible physical objects
- give extended practice of methods
- build confidence with numbers
- develop a sense of number values
- gain an understanding that numbers can be manipulated and rounded up or down for easier calculation
- develop reliable methods of working.

Encourage playing card games and dominoes to see number patterns (Figure 3.7).

Number patterns making 10

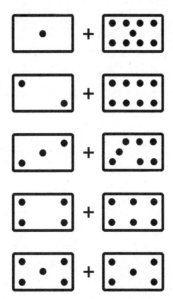

FIGURE 3.7 SOME SIMPLE NUMBER PATTERNS

Computer games

There are many interactive number games available, and students generally enjoy playing them. The difficulty levels can be graded, they are non-judgemental and students can progress.

Assistive technology

There are now specific maths IT support programmes available for use in class and in exams; these allow voice-to-text and vice versa (see resources list for this chapter).

Confidence

This is probably most important of all and it comes gradually and with success. There will be a noticeable reduction in anxiety if the student is given coping strategies to remember information, guidelines to follow and lots of practice.

A teacher who is approachable, fun, relaxed and adaptable can make all the difference.

KEY POINTS

- -

- Dyscalculia is a recognised SpLD.
- It is a problem with numbers and arithmetic.
- It affects about 6 per cent of the population.
- With the correct support students with dyscalculia can learn to compensate for their difficulties.
- Multisensory teaching and solid, everyday examples are helpful.
- Sensitive classroom teachers can make a huge difference.

- -

CHAPTER 4

Dysgraphia

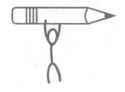

* ★ What is dysgraphia?
* ★ How is dysgraphia diagnosed?
* ★ How can I spot a student with dysgraphia?
* ★ Common strengths
* ★ Common indicators (downsides)
* ★ Overall approach
* ★ Classroom strategies
* ★ Individual support
* ★ Key points

WHAT IS DYSGRAPHIA?

Dysgraphia is a lesser known Specific Learning Difference (SpLD) which affects *handwriting and converting thoughts to written words.*

People with dysgraphia are within the normal intelligence range but they struggle to put their ideas down clearly and coherently on paper. Their writing may be untidy or illegible despite considerable effort, and there is a disparity between ideas and understanding expressed orally and those presented in writing. Their reading ability is normal. Spelling may be affected, but this is not always the case.

Dysgraphia is thought to affect up to 10 per cent of the population to varying degrees (Cleveland Clinic 2022) and it can affect both boys and girls. It often occurs with other SpLDs but not always. There is a tendency for it to run in families.

The American Psychiatric Association (2013) describes dysgraphia as 'impairment in written expression' and 'writing skills (that)...are substantially below those expected given the person's...age, measured intelligence, and age-appropriate education'.

WHERE DOES THE NAME COME FROM?

Dys comes from the Greek word meaning *difficulty*. *Graphia* comes from the Greek word meaning *writing*. So dysgraphia means difficulty with handwriting.

There are three forms of dysgraphia and the symptoms and effective treatment may vary depending on the cause.

- *Spatial dysgraphia:* poor visual processing and understanding of space. This causes difficulty writing on lines and spacing letters. Drawing and colouring will also be affected. Both copied and original work are untidy and may be illegible. Spelling is normal.
- *Motor dysgraphia:* poor fine motor control of hand and wrist muscles, which makes writing difficult and tiring and generally results in untidy or illegible writing even when copying. Spelling is not affected.
- *Processing dysgraphia (sometimes called dyslexic dysgraphia):* difficulty visualising the appearance of the letters in a word, which results in the letters being malformed and in the wrong order when written. Original written work is illegible but copied work is better. Spelling is poor.

Individuals may have one form of dysgraphia or a combination.

HOW IS DYSGRAPHIA DIAGNOSED?

Typically a diagnosis of dysgraphia is made by a specialist teacher or educational psychologist with input from a physiotherapist or occupational therapist.

HOW CAN I SPOT A STUDENT WITH DYSGRAPHIA?

The student is probably good with the spoken word but consistently hands in work that looks untidy and is well below the quality that you would expect. If you watch them write, you may notice that the process can be laborious and their posture and pen grip look awkward. They are slow to copy from the board or from a book and they may complain of an aching hand.

COMMON STRENGTHS

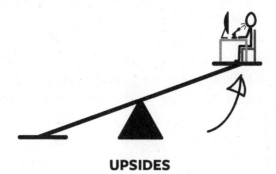

UPSIDES

- Normal or high intelligence.
- No social or behavioural difficulties.
- Generally no other underlying academic problems.
- May be very good orally and come up with interesting and unusual ideas.
- Creative and imaginative, good in visual arts or design.
- Computer-based skills often very good.

- May be talented in music, drama, sport or other areas of the curriculum not requiring writing.

COMMON INDICATORS (DOWNSIDES)

DOWNSIDES

Spatial dysgraphia

- May not write on the lines.
- May not able to follow margins.
- Can have difficulty organising words from left to right.
- May leave inconsistent space between words and letters; may be too close or too far apart.
- Letters may be of irregular size, shape and slant.
- May have trouble reading maps or following directions.
- There may be difficulty with drawing and colouring.
- May have difficulty laying out arithmetic answers or doing geometry.

Motor dysgraphia

- Writing may be very poor and difficult to read.
- May be very slow at writing, either original writing or copying from a board or book.
- Can get tired quickly when writing.
- May suffer from painful cramps while writing for extended periods.
- May have an abnormal pen grip and hand position.
- May have an unusual wrist, body or paper position.

- May struggle to use mathematical instruments.
- May have difficulty drawing graphs.
- Other skills involving fine motor control can be affected, such as manipulating science apparatus.

Processing dysgraphia

- The physical act of writing takes a lot of concentration so their ability to process information at the same time as writing is affected.
- May have difficulty remembering how to form some letters.
- Some letters may be unfinished or backwards.
- There may be a mixture of small and capital letters on the same line.
- There may be a mixture of printing and cursive writing on the same line.
- Letters or whole words may be omitted, or letters or words repeated.
- There may be poor and erratic spelling and punctuation.
- May put in the wrong word in a sentence.
- May have difficulty organising thoughts logically on paper; may lose train of thought.
- May miss out key information.
- May write long, rambling sentences with repetition.
- May be very slow to think and compose sentences.
- May underperform in tests and exams.

Other indicators

- Fluent when speaking but stilted language and limited ideas expressed on paper.
- May say the words out loud when writing.

Emotional responses

- May suffer from disappointment as written work takes a lot of effort and will always look poor.
- Written tasks can cause extreme frustration and stress.
- May fall behind academically as all written work takes much longer so they may not finish what is required in an allotted time.
- May try to avoid written tasks altogether or write as little as possible.
- May have low self-esteem.

OVERALL APPROACH

- Show that you appreciate that writing is difficult and the student is not being sloppy or lazy when written work looks untidy.
- Make it clear that you think they are intelligent and capable of achieving a high standard academically.
- Be aware that the act of writing needs extra concentration and time and that a student will not be able to write and process information simultaneously.
- Consider alternative ways of recording information to avoid too much handwriting.
- Be positive and cheerful and try to boost their self-belief.

CLASSROOM STRATEGIES

Use of technology

The use of a computer and keyboard has benefited many students with dysgraphia and allows work to be well presented and legible. If possible allow students to use a keyboard for longer pieces of work and in class.

Today voice recognition software is increasingly important and has been shown to make a huge difference. Taking away the need to struggle with writing allows people who have dysgraphia to be free to think creatively and produce work that reflects their ability.

These programmes can now be used in exams (see Chapter 13). However, in lessons it may not always be feasible to use IT and so the following suggestions may helpful to teachers.

During lessons

- Reduce the amount of written work that is required to allow students with dysgraphia to keep up with the academic content of your subject.
- Give out printed notes so they have a correct and legible copy to learn from. They could highlight key points.
- Find out if students can sound-record part of the lesson.
- If printed notes have gaps to fill in by hand, make sure that the spaces are large enough to accommodate larger or poorly positioned writing.
- Consider increasing the paper size and use double spacing,
- Give out sets of short, closed questions to answer rather than instructions such as 'write a paragraph on'.
- Graph paper can be useful to help with the layout of mathematical calculations.
- Use paper with raised margins or lines to aid layout.
- Check that the student is keeping up with the pace of the class if writing is involved.
- Encourage students to rub their hands together or shake their hands downwards periodically to relieve tension and improve blood flow. Doing small push-ups from a sitting position can bring some relief.
- Allow extra time for written tests.

Sitting position

- Try to ensure that the student sits in an upright position with their feet on the ground.

- A writing slope may also be helpful (Figure 4.1). This enables a student to write with the paper placed at a slight angle. These are available commercially. A posture pack may also be beneficial. This is a wedge-shaped pillow that helps to maintain a good sitting position to aid writing.

FIGURE 4.1 WRITING POSITION USING A WRITING SLOPE

- Make sure that they are not too close to other students as they may need elbow room.
- If the student sits near the front, you can keep an eye on their progress.

Homework

- Try to be imaginative and flexible.
- Students with dysgraphia write more slowly than others if they are writing by hand so they will not be able to produce as much homework in a set time.
- Allow the use of paper with larger line spaces or raised lines.
- Allow the use of technology if it is feasible – either a word processor or voice-to-text software.
- Is there another way that students can present their work?

For notes on organising thoughts on paper for essays and projects see Chapter 12.

Marking

- Mark written work for content not appearance.
- Try to be encouraging and make constructive suggestions.
- Acknowledge effort and improvement.

Tests and exams (see Chapter 13)

- Alternative ways of testing, such as oral tests, multiple-choice questions, or giving a short presentation could be alternatives to conventional exams.
- Special arrangements may be in place for public exams. Make sure that you are aware of these. Students could qualify for extra time or can use a word processor or voice-to-text software. If this is the case, they will need to practise this in school exams and tests.

INDIVIDUAL SUPPORT

Students may benefit from individual support and advice from an *occupational therapist* or *specialist learning support teacher*. They can give helpful, practical advice and introduce the student to a range of products and strategies.

Special paper for students with dysgraphia is available commercially both for writing and for maths.

Exercises

- Hand exercises can improve fine motor control.
- Writing warm-up exercises may be helpful. Rubbing the hands together or shaking them can also relieve muscle tension.
- Extra instruction and practice at writing – some people with dysgraphia can develop a nice cursive writing style which they can use if they have to. It takes a lot of energy and

concentration to write nicely and it is very slow, so it would not be their chosen method but is useful at times.

- Pen hold – very often people with dysgraphia have an incorrect pen grip or they grip too hard. Training may be needed to adapt to a more conventional grip such as the tripod grip shown in Figure 4.2.

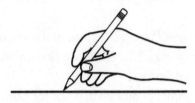

FIGURE 4.2 TRIPOD PENCIL HOLD

- Special shaped pens or rubber pencil grippers (Figure 4.3) are available and some students find them helpful (see resources list for this chapter).

FIGURE 4.3 RUBBER PENCIL GRIP

Vision

It is worth checking for visual tracking problems as it could be that the student's eyes are not working together properly. A specialist behavioural optometrist would advise and might suggest some form of vision therapy.

KEY POINTS

- -

- Dysgraphia is a recognised SpLD.
- It is a difficulty with the physical act of handwriting and with organising thoughts on paper.

- Students have normal to above-average IQ and reading ability. Spelling may be affected but this is not always the case.
- Early diagnosis and writing therapy can help greatly but the difficulty will not be 'cured'.
- Teachers should be sympathetic and mark for content not appearance.
- Students will need extra time for handwritten assignments.
- The use of technology will transform the quality of work produced.

Dyspraxia/Developmental Coordination Disorder (DCD)

★ What is dyspraxia/DCD?

★ How is dyspraxia/DCD diagnosed?

★ How can I spot a student with dyspraxia?

★ Common strengths

★ Common indicators (downsides)

★ Overall approach

★ Classroom strategies

★ Outside the classroom

★ Individual support

★ Key points

WHAT IS DYSPRAXIA/DCD?

People with dyspraxia/DCD have *difficulty with muscular coordination and movement*. The muscles themselves are normal but dyspraxia is the result of a 'brain-wiring' (neuro-biological) difference. Fine motor skills, which control precision movements, especially of the hands, or gross motor skills which control whole body movements, can be affected, and so can speech.

Executive function skills (see page 21) may also be affected so children with dyspraxia may have problems with organisation, short-term memory, planning and social interaction. They may also have problems with speech and language.

Motor coordination difficulties + organisation difficulties = dyspraxia.

Dyspraxia occurs on a continuum from mild to severe and it does not affect overall intelligence.

The cause of dyspraxia is unknown and there may be several contributory factors. In some cases there is evidence that it may run in families. It is thought that up to 5 per cent of children in the UK may have some degree of dyspraxia. It occurs in boys and girls although currently greater numbers of boys are diagnosed at school age (Dyspraxia Foundation 2015).

WHERE DOES THE NAME COME FROM?

Dys comes from the Greek word meaning *difficulty*. *Praxia* from the Greek word meaning *doing*. So dyspraxia means *difficulty doing*.

Developmental coordination disorder (DCD) is another term used for dyspraxia, and the two terms are often used interchangeably. The term 'developmental' means that the person is born with this difference and it does not occur as a result of injury or illness, so it is distinct from coordination problems caused by conditions such as a stroke or cerebral palsy. DCD is therefore the preferred term used medically. But the more usual term used in schools is dyspraxia, so for simplicity, the term 'dyspraxia' will be used throughout this chapter.

HOW IS DYSPRAXIA/DCD DIAGNOSED?

Dyspraxia is a medical diagnosis generally made by a paediatrician, neurologist or GP. It is important to have the correct medical diagnosis as some of the coordination difficulties seen in dyspraxia may also occur in other medical conditions. Once dyspraxia is identified then the correct support can be put in place, often involving physiotherapy, occupational therapy or in some cases speech therapy.

HOW CAN I SPOT A STUDENT WITH DYSPRAXIA?

Look for the student who may arrive at your lesson flustered and slightly late. They might drop things, lose or forget equipment, fidget or fall. They can contribute well in class but their written work is untidy and disorganised and doesn't seem to do justice to their ability. They might struggle in sports lessons.

COMMON STRENGTHS

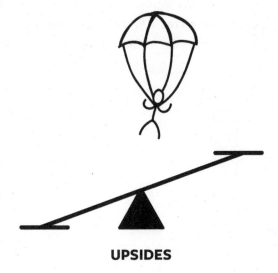

UPSIDES

- Lateral, imaginative, 'outside the box' thinker.
- Creative; may shine at design, use of colour and textures, photography.
- Able to recall events from long ago in detail.
- May have a special interest in certain topics and be very knowledgeable about them.
- Imaginative; good at writing, stories, plays or poems.
- Good at literature or poetry.
- ICT skills may be very good.
- Determined.
- Good orally and may excel in debating, telling stories or acting.
- Good with younger children or animals.
- Honest.

A VIEW FROM THE INSIDE

Lying diagonally in a parallel universe means that we have a brilliant and unusual slant on life. We see things that others can't, and for this reason I feel that we are very lucky to be dyspraxic.

From Victoria Biggs's book Caged in Chaos: A Dyspraxic Guide to Breaking Free, *a funny but poignant autobiography describing her time at a British boarding school*

COMMON INDICATORS (DOWNSIDES)

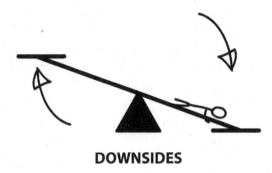

DOWNSIDES

Students with dyspraxia will show some of the indicators listed but not all of them. Remember that some students may also have other Specific Learning Differences as well.

Gross motor skills

- May have poor coordination; may appear clumsy.
- Liable to trip, spill or drop things.
- May fidget in class.
- Spatial awareness may be poor, liable to bump into people or objects.
- May have difficulty with games due to coordination problems, including catching a ball, balancing, gymnastics, riding a bicycle.
- May have an untidy and scruffy appearance.

Fine motor skills

- May have poor handwriting and immature drawing skills. (See also motor dysgraphia in Chapter 4.)
- May have difficulty using instruments in subjects such as geometry, science, cookery and design technology.
- May be slow to dress – problems with buttons, ties and shoelaces.

Organisational skills (see Chapter 12)

May have difficulty with the following:

- following timetables
- time keeping – often arrives late and flustered
- allocating time to tasks
- sense of direction and finding their way to places
- keeping files, books and equipment in order
- bringing correct equipment to lessons
- keeping notes in order.

Short-term memory

May have difficulty with the following:

- remembering a set of instructions or a routine
- recalling names of people and places
- remembering codes, phone numbers or where lessons take place
- remembering to do homework or to hand it in
- retaining numbers while working out maths problems, so may struggle with mental arithmetic
- memorising times tables
- revising quickly – it takes longer to learn because information must be stored in the long-term memory
- retaining information – must re-learn the material regularly.

Tests and exams (see Chapter 13)

- Handwriting may be poor; and may deteriorate during exam due to fatigue and time pressure.
- Written work may include frequent crossing out.
- Essay answers may be disorganised as thoughts are disjointed.
- Timing exams – may spend too long on one question or attempt the wrong number of questions.
- Interpreting questions – may take them too literally or not give enough detail in answers.

- Answers are often shorter than expected. This can be due to the act of writing being tiring or because the subtle inferences of the question are missed.

Sense perception

Students with dyspraxia may be over-sensitive (hypersensitive) to some incoming stimuli (light, sound, touch, smell, taste) or they may be under-sensitive (hyposensitive). This can affect their behaviour, school life and their ability to concentrate. (See Chapter 9 on sensory processing disorder.)

Social and emotional

- May be less emotionally mature than peer group.
- May show poor interpersonal skills.
- May have difficulty reading body language.
- May not easily be able to pick up implied information.
- May interpret of language literally.
- May be unaware of the norms of personal distance; might stand too close or too far away from others.
- May not 'fit in with the crowd'.
- May want to have friends but unsure how to engage on a light social level.
- Can find socialising tiring; may wish to have some quiet time alone.
- May become isolated and a 'loner'. This is increased by a poor ability at team sport which they will try to avoid.
- May interrupt conversations.
- Some students will compensate by immersing themselves in computer games or books to avoid social contact and possible rejection.

Emilie was never without a book, even at meal times. She found the company of fictional characters much less tiring than trying to make conversation with other students.

Author

Depression

This is a common problem for students with dyspraxia. It can result from:

- feeling clumsy and awkward
- embarrassment and physical pain when accidents occur
- not being able to excel in school sports
- written work looking scruffy and receiving negative feedback from teachers
- feeling undervalued for intellect or potential
- low self-esteem
- friendship issues, may be teased or bullied
- social isolation.

Tiredness

A lot of extra effort has to go into performing physical actions, remembering things and dealing with social encounters. The result is that students with dyspraxia often get very tired coping with a school day. They really value some quiet time if it is possible.

A VIEW FROM THE INSIDE

Imagine riding a bicycle with loose handlebars. To ride it you would need to be constantly correcting the steering as every bump sends the front wheel off course. You could never relax and it would be very tiring. This is what dyspraxia is like for me. Simple actions sometimes need an inordinate amount of concentration and it is hard not to feel a degree of inadequacy when others can be seen to accomplish these tasks so effortlessly.

John, student with dyspraxia

OVERALL APPROACH

- Students with dyspraxia often say they feel 'clumsy and stupid', so show that you understand dyspraxia.
- Be clear that you value their intellect and contributions to the class and that you do expect them to do well.
- Work with them and discuss what techniques help them to learn the best. Be open to ideas from the students. They are the experts in dealing with dyspraxia and they can help you come up with effective strategies.

CLASSROOM STRATEGIES

Motor difficulties

- Anticipate potential accidents: make sure the students are aware of steps or other obstacles near your classroom.
- Keep the classroom floor clear of clutter – school bags, books or coats on the floor are trip hazards. Particular care will be needed for practical subjects.
- If you teach a practical subject, accidents will happen! Try substituting plastic for glass vessels and go through safety rules carefully with the class. If a breakage or spillage occurs, keep calm and be aware of the procedure to follow. Keep the students as safe as possible.
- Seating – are the seats in your classroom easy to balance on? Science labs are often the worst as students can be expected to balance on high stools. Is there an alternative? Ideally the

student should be sitting upright with their back supported and with their feet placed firmly on the ground (Figure 5.1).

- A writing slope or seat wedge might also help (see Chapter 4, Figure 4.1).

CASE STUDY: DYSPRAXIA

When he was a young teenager the worst time in the week for Francis was chemistry. He was clumsy and very worried about knocking equipment over, spilling liquids, breaking apparatus bumping into others and on one embarrassing occasion he had even fallen off the stool that he had to perch on throughout the lesson. The teacher was not amused and thought that he was just messing about. He did not like the feel of the material of the shared school lab coats. No one wanted to work with him.

Once his dyspraxia and SPD were diagnosed things began to improve. He was allowed to sit at the end of a row, making accidents less likely, and the floor became a bag-free zone reducing trips. In time, his stool was replaced by a more stable chair. Plastic equipment placed on a tray made spills less likely and he usually worked with a partner who was dextrous and he was the recorder of results for them both. He was allowed to use IT for written work and graphs so his written work improved greatly.

His natural intelligence and ability to grasp concepts and 3D structures mean that he is now really enjoying biochemistry at University. He has his own lab coat in a material that he likes and he hopes to get a Nobel Prize one day!

Takeaway idea: *Allow the student to overcome physical barriers to learning and they will often thrive.*

FIGURE 5.1 AN IDEAL SITTING POSITION

- Let students with dyspraxia sit near the front. This means that they can see the board clearly and you can observe their progress. They can feel more involved in the lesson and are less likely to get distracted. They are also better sitting at the end of a row rather than in the middle.
- Fidgeting – if they are jiggling it can be to maintain balance and get muscle feedback. Try not to get irritated. They may benefit from moving around the room periodically.
- Something to fiddle with – a stress ball or equivalent can be useful and it often aids concentration. It might also stop them from tapping with a pencil, which annoys everyone.
- Using equipment – fine motor control difficulties can make it hard to use instruments requiring dexterity. Try to anticipate problems and avoid embarrassment. Special equipment can be provided if the school budget allows. Larger or Easi-Grip® scissors, more stable containers or adapted geometry instruments could make life easier.

A VIEW FROM THE INSIDE

When you are perching on a high stool with no back or arms, you may be so busy trying to keep your balance that you can't listen to the teacher.

Victoria Biggs, from her book Caged in Chaos:
A Dyspraxic Guide to Breaking Free

Giving notes

As hand coordination is affected by dyspraxia, writing is difficult and tiring so there is an overlap with dysgraphia (see Chapter 4). Physically writing notes may be exhausting and the result could be inaccurate and illegible.

- Reduce the quantity of handwriting required as much as possible. Give out printed notes possibly with gaps to fill in so the student can keep up with the lesson and stay engaged.
- Remember, the student is concentrating on their handwriting they will not be able to process or remember the content.

Writing and presentation (see Chapter 4)

- Pens and pencils with different grips, non-slip rulers and other adapted mathematical instruments can be purchased.
- Using large paper or squared paper can help with layout.
- Check the student's written work regularly for accuracy.
- Students should continue to practise handwriting and fine motor skills even though it is difficult.

Use of computers and assistive technology

The quality of the work produced using technology is a much better reflection of the student's ability. Students with dyspraxia should be encouraged to practise their computer skills as often as possible.

- Using a keyboard or voice-to-text software removes the physical difficulty of writing. Students can then concentrate on the content of what they are saying and their flow of thoughts. Often the result is much more mature and insightful.
- Paragraphs can also be moved about electronically and this helps with essay organisation.
- Work can be illustrated with graphs and diagrams.
- Is it possible for students to sound-record class notes and then convert them to written notes using voice-to-text software?

Multisensory teaching (see Chapter 2)

- Try to reinforce your lessons in a multisensory way. Include visual, audio and kinaesthetic input and vary the activities.
- Lessons are more memorable if active participation is involved.
- Reducing the time spent writing enables students to participate more fully.

Working with others

Working in pairs often works better if you choose pairs with complementary skills. They can divide the tasks, but make sure that both students are actively involved.

Group work can be challenging for students with dyspraxia but it can work well with a little 'stage management'. You should pick the groups to balance talents and personalities. This also removes any embarrassment about not being chosen by peers. Ascribe different roles within the groups and watch out for unkindness or bullying. Change the groupings in different lessons.

Sometimes students with dyspraxia have their own very creative and different ideas and enjoy an opportunity to work alone and follow their own interests. I feel that this is OK on occasion, but not as the norm, and it is also better if some others wish to go solo.

Organisational skills

Disorganisation is an integral part of dyspraxia and this can seriously affect progress at school. Strategies for compensating and finding coping mechanisms are covered in Chapter 12.

Homework

- Give this out early in the lesson.
- Be very clear – it's best to give written as well as spoken instructions.
- Could they dictate the homework into a mobile phone?
- Does the school have an intranet system where homework is placed?
- If students have copied homework down, check that it is correct.
- Give clear instructions, including the time you would expect them to spend on the work, when it should be completed, where it should be handed in and whether it can it be done on a computer.
- Show clearly how you would like a piece of work laid out. Instructions such as 'underline with a ruler', 'this diagram should fill half a page', 'draw a ruled box in pencil around a table' are helpful.
- Consider giving a larger version of a question sheet, especially if it has gaps to fill in or space for working. Do not be tempted to give out reduced-size question sheets in order to save paper.
- Set different, more creative, types of homework from time to time.

Marking homework

- Mark for content not presentation.
- Be encouraging, acknowledge and praise progress and effort.
- Try to give a useful and constructive comment for the student to think about next time.
- Decide what is important to correct this time.

Your support is valued by students with dyspraxia. Try to be consistent, approachable and open to ideas. Celebrate successes when they occur and you will have already gone a long way to making a big difference.

OUTSIDE THE CLASSROOM

There will be many other difficulties facing students with dyspraxia around school. It is useful to be aware of these even if they might not be directly relevant to your subject.

Games lessons
These can be a nightmare for students with dyspraxia for several reasons.

Changing clothes takes much longer and may be stressful, especially if the changing room is crowded: finding kit from bags or lockers, opening lockers with keys or codes, fumbling with buttons and shoelaces with time pressure and poor dexterity can all be very difficult and cause anxiety.

Strategies for games lessons:

- Allow the student go a little early to get changed at the beginning and end of games sessions:
  - The changing room is not crowded, reducing the chance of kit getting lost.
  - It decreases overall stress.
  - Students are less likely to be late for the next lesson.
- Parents could be encouraged to provide clothes that are easier to put on, such as having Velcro® on shoes or shirts rather than laces or buttons.
- All kit should be clearly marked, preferably in large clear letters or with colour coding so it can be identified quickly.
- Spare kit could be available to borrow.

Team games are often genuinely difficult, especially if they involve throwing and catching a ball:

- The student will be conscious of letting others down.
- They are likely to be the last to be picked by peers so try to avoid this situation.

Strategies for team games:

- Teachers pick the teams to balance the skills.
- Offer some individual tuition with ball skills carried out by a teacher or physiotherapist.
- Students have a role – they may enjoy being part of the team in another capacity: scorer, line judge, time keeper, photographer? Being an official gives a genuine sports role and they can travel to fixtures as a valued member of the team.

As the student gets older they may wish to pursue other sports and activities which are more suited to their skills. Swimming, line dancing, running, martial arts, Pilates and kayaking have been recommended. These will help develop strength, improve coordination and increase confidence.

I have happy memories of taking a group of students for a weekly sailing lesson. The group included Olivia, who was an outgoing girl with dyspraxia, and her best friend Annie, who was an excellent sailor and more serious. Annie's skill and Olivia's enthusiasm and sense of fun made them a great partnership. A good time was had by all but we did have to allow an extra 15 minutes at the end to extricate Olivia from her wetsuit!

Author

Lunch and break time

Lunch and break times are unstructured and often unsupervised. They can be unhappy and stressful for students with dyspraxia as teasing and bullying can occur.

- Lunch queues – these can be busy and crowded, and carrying trays of food can be very perilous for students with dyspraxia.
- Could they have a buddy to carry the tray? Nothing is more embarrassing in a crowded dining room than dropping a full tray of lunch!
- Can they go in to lunch a little early, with a friend? Or eat in a quieter location?
- They may eat lunch more slowly and more messily than their peers. If they are not too embarrassed to use a napkin it can save them from having a shirt with food stains for the afternoon.
- Is a packed lunch an option?
- Lunch break – going to clubs or societies is a way of 'escaping' unstructured time and pursuing a hobby, and of having a role within the school.

A VIEW FROM THE INSIDE

At secondary school my son always took refuge in the library at lunch time.

Mother of boy with dyspraxia

Social inclusion

Social situations can be challenging for students with dyspraxia and they can become isolated and depressed. Assure them that there are many options and valuable roles for them to fill.

- Encourage them to go to interest clubs and activities within school. It is much easier to make friends through a common interest.
- Could they be a photographer or reporter for the school journal?
- School drama or music productions offer a variety of

roles, either on stage or behind the scenes. Being part of a production gives a sense of unity and a common purpose and creates a social network.

- Involvement in charity work, either fundraising or community action, can be fun.
- Could they assist with activities for younger children?

INDIVIDUAL SUPPORT

A *designated adult mentor*, who sees the student individually on a regular basis, can make a big difference. The mentor can provide support for the student, deal with difficulties as they arise and help to increase their self-confidence by praising their achievements and progress. Often a mentor can act as a 'go-between', relaying the student's worries to their class teachers and vice versa.

A specialist learning support teacher provides tailored academic support for the student and advice for teachers. They may also work on fine motor skills and handwriting and help with organisation.

A *physiotherapist* may work regularly with the student to support coordination.

The *sports department* may put in extra sessions to practise coordination skills.

Social skills

A mentor can also be helpful for reinforcing topics covered in PSHE (personal, social and health education) lessons and talking about areas which can cause difficulty or embarrassment:

- how to engage in conversation
- how to interpret body language
- inference and implied meaning
- personal hygiene

- personal space.

Organisational skills and time planning (see Chapter 12)

Students might need help to find coping strategies for organisation that work best for them. They will need continued support throughout school, including the sixth form.

Help with time-management skills, how to set work priorities and meeting deadlines will be important.

Exams and revision (see Chapter 13)

Students who have dyspraxia may qualify for special arrangements in public exams. These could include extra time, using a word processor, using voice-to-text software or having a scribe to write for them.

The school SENCO (special educational needs coordinator) and exams officer are responsible for ensuring that the necessary arrangements are in place.

KEY POINTS

- -

- Dyspraxia is a recognised SpLD.
- It causes difficulties with movement and coordination.
- Short-term memory, organisation and social interaction can also be affected.
- Dyspraxia affects around 5 per cent of the population and is more often diagnosed earlier in boys.
- Students with dyspraxia have many talents and skills but may be socially isolated.
- Friendships occur most easily if there is a common interest.
- Students benefit from using a computer or voice recognition software for written work.
- Supportive teachers can make a big difference.

- -

CHAPTER 6

Attention Deficit Hyperactivity Disorder (ADHD)

★ What is ADHD?

★ How is ADHD diagnosed?

★ How is ADHD treated?

★ How can I spot a student with ADHD?

★ Common strengths

★ Common indicators (downsides)

★ Overall approach

★ Classroom strategies

★ Whole-school approach

★ Outside the classroom

★ Individual support

★ Key points

WHAT IS ADHD?

People with ADHD often show three behavioural indicators:

- inattention
- hyperactivity
- impulsiveness.

ADHD is a brain-chemistry (neuro-biological) disorder. It cannot be cured but it can respond to medicine, behavioural therapy and lifestyle changes. It is thought to affect up to 5 per cent of children and young people and is the most common behavioural disorder in the UK (NHS Choices n.d.). The severity varies over a continuum from mild to severe.

ADHD often runs in families, suggesting that there is a genetic link, but it can also be affected by environmental and lifestyle factors. It does not affect the overall intelligence of the individual, although it can impair their progress unless carefully controlled.

Many people with ADHD also suffer from other learning differences, such as dyslexia or an autism spectrum disorder (ASD). They may also have additional problems such as insomnia and anxiety.

WHERE DOES THE NAME COME FROM?

The American Psychiatric Association adopted the name 'attention deficit hyperactivity disorder' (ADHD) in 1994 in its *Diagnostic and Statistical Manual*.

Definition

ADHD is 'a persistent pattern of inattention and/or hyperactivity-impulsivity that interferes with development, has symptoms presenting in two or more settings (e.g. at home and school), and negatively impacts directly on social, academic or occupational functioning' (American Psychiatric Association 2013).

There are three types of ADHD with differing symptoms:

- Predominantly inattentive ADHD – diagnosed more frequently in girls
- Predominantly hyperactive/impulsive ADHD
- Combined ADHD – inattentive and hyperactive/impulsive most common, diagnosed more often in boys.

The old term attention deficit disorder (ADD) has now been replaced with predominantly inattentive ADHD.

BRAIN CHEMISTRY AND ADHD

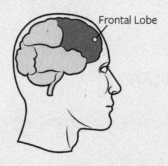

Frontal Lobe

The front part of the brain (frontal lobe) controls our rational and logical behaviour. It enables us to think before we act and to learn from experience. It also allows us to inhibit certain emotional responses, to modify our behaviour and to prevent us from taking risks that are unwise. The lobes are also the site of our personality, goal setting, planning and making us who we are. Brain cells communicate using chemicals called neurotransmitters. It has been shown that people with ADHD have less neurotransmitter activity than usual in the frontal lobe region. This produces more risk taking, spontaneity and a lack of concentration.

HOW IS ADHD DIAGNOSED?

ADHD in children and adolescents is a medical diagnosis. It is carried out by a *specialist paediatrician* or *child psychiatrist*. This would follow a referral from a GP. The range of indicators must have been present for at least six months and impact adversely on daily life in two settings, usually home and school. The symptoms must have been present before the age of 12 years and are unlikely to be explained by other factors, such as a mental disorder, anxiety, mood disorder, or by other medical treatment or changes in home environment

In the UK, diagnosis often involves the Child and Adolescent Mental Health Services (CAMHS); these services support young people experiencing poor mental health, or difficult feelings or experiences.

Getting a diagnosis is a lengthy process and schools should make adjustments to support students if ADHD is suspected and not always wait until a final diagnosis

HOW IS ADHD TREATED?

ADHD is a medical condition and so the child's GP or paediatrician should be monitoring the student's treatment. Here, I will merely briefly mention the current trends in treatment.

- *Managing the student's environment* and recognising stress points and triggers leading to meltdowns. This can be done in collaboration between home and school.
- *Controlling diet and reducing sugar intake* has been shown to help keep children calmer in some cases, but the evidence is not conclusive. Food colourings and additives may also be implicated.
- *Relaxation techniques* can help.
- *Cognitive behavioural therapy (CBT)* has also been shown to

be useful as it teaches the student how to recognise symptoms and manage their behaviour.

- *Medications* (*neurostimulants*) are sometimes used as these can improve concentration by increasing brain activity in the frontal lobe area. This produces calmer behaviour and greater focus, allowing the student to concentrate and learn.

HOW CAN I SPOT A STUDENT WITH ADHD?

It is easier to spot students who display hyperactivity and impulsiveness. They are probably the ones who cannot sit still, who call out in class and are constantly demanding your attention. They can be bright, sparky and innovative but always seem to be attention seeking and need frequent disciplining. They could act as the class jester if bored, but they can also become angry or upset and erupt into an emotional outburst of temper.

The inattentive form of ADHD is much harder to detect. Students may appear to be rather dreamy and do not listen properly when you talk to them. They are disorganised and do not seem to take information in very well. They may avoid hard tasks and feel that they cannot cope.

Students with all types ADHD often really want to do well and please the teacher but they struggle with organisation and 'getting things right'. Their written work can be inadequate or incomplete, although they may have started out with great ideas. They may frequently argue and fall out with their peers, but this can sometimes be due to provocation and teasing.

Depression is a common problem among these young people, as they feel that they will never be able to keep friends and do well at school.

COMMON STRENGTHS

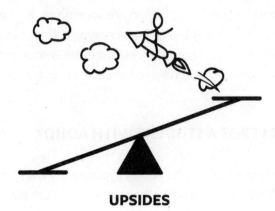

UPSIDES

- Great enthusiasm.
- Innovative ideas.
- Lots of energy.
- Different perspective as a lateral thinker.
- Charismatic and engaging.
- Fearless. Will delight in trying new things; loves 'having a go'.
- Will volunteer readily.
- Can be excellent at acting, dance or sport.
- Often kind, friendly and outgoing.
- Can be very good with younger children.
- May rise to a challenge if given some responsibility.
- Generally wants to do well and have friends.
- May have a strong sense of justice and fairness.
- May have a passion for a particular topic, sport or hobby.

COMMON INDICATORS (DOWNSIDES)

DOWNSIDES

Inattention

- Can be easily distracted.
- May have short attention span; moving from one activity to another.
- May have difficulty remaining focused.
- May not listen properly.
- May make careless mistakes.
- Organisation – may lose things, arrive late, forget to hand in work.
- May have poor short-term memory.
- May have difficulty following instructions.
- May appear rather detached and absent-minded.
- May have a tendency to avoid tasks needing sustained mental effort.
- May fail to complete tasks despite good intentions.

Hyperactivity

- May fidget with hands and jiggle legs when sitting.
- May appear restless and distracted.
- May get out of seat frequently in class.
- Can be silly and show off.
- May run or climb at inappropriate times (in older children this can be replaced by a general restlessness).
- May talk excessively.
- May be unable to relax and be calm.

- May have a chaotic manner; for example, arriving late without the correct books or equipment.

Impulsiveness

- May shout out in class.
- May be impatient.
- May be excitable.
- May find it difficult to wait for a turn.
- May interrupt and intrude on other people's conversations.
- Can be anxious and agitated.
- May react emotionally, not rationally.
- Can become angry and aggressive or tearful.
- May be a risk taker; defiant.
- May always be looking for the most exciting thing to do.

Executive function difficulties

Executive function skills enable us to organise and plan activities, to think logically and to carry out tasks successfully to completion. These functions work together to help us to reach personal goals, learn from mistakes and override impulsive behaviour.

Students with ADHD often struggle to develop these skills and so they may have difficulty with the following activities at school:

- remembering details or instructions, and retaining numbers long enough to carry out a calculation
- focusing and sustaining attention
- organising, planning and prioritising
- estimating how much time a project will take to complete
- learning from experience and reflecting with hindsight
- regulating behaviour by thinking about consequences
- making rational decisions
- completing tasks – they often have great ideas, but are unable to persevere and complete them

- reacting logically rather than emotionally – this can cause issues with friendships and relations with teachers
- inhibiting certain impulsive behaviour patterns
- 'defusing' the build-up of emotion, resulting in temper outbreaks.

CASE STUDY: ADHD

Andrew was a lively boy who was full of bright ideas but somehow always seemed to end up in trouble with school and having arguments with his friends. At the age of 14 years he was diagnosed with ADHD and given medication to control his hyperactive and impulsive behaviour. He began to do better academically and was able to focus more on sport, which he was good at. His love was swimming and he joined a local club. With daily training sessions before school and swimming fixtures at weekends he found that much of his manic behaviour stopped and he could reduce his dependence on medication, which he disliked taking. His life became more balanced, school work improved and he began to swim for his county.

Takeaway idea: *Physical challenges can be very helpful for students who have ADHD, especially when they involve discipline and training.*

OVERALL APPROACH

Your attitude is important. These students can have exciting and interesting ideas, lots of enthusiasm and an unusual and original approach. However, they may need careful control and patient but firm discipline. They may be disorganised and behind with their work or they may have mislaid it completely. In class they might shout out, leap out of their seat and disrupt lessons by demanding attention. This combination of qualities makes them both challenging and rewarding to teach.

If they have the inattentive form of ADHD they will be less disruptive, but they can appear to be rude, uninterested and not listening to you. It is important that you try to keep them engaged and motivated, and don't take it personally.

Remember that most students with ADHD want to do well and that they are sad and upset when things go wrong and their behaviour lets them down. You can help them a great deal by showing understanding and being positive and proactive in your approach.

- Let them know that you believe in them and in their ability.
- Have clear and fair discipline rules.
- Be approachable but firm.
- Try to be in consistent your own behaviour and demeanour.
- Let them know that they can come and seek individual help from you.
- Remain upbeat and cheerful.
- Show that you care and remember to smile.

CLASSROOM STRATEGIES

- Always start the lessons the same way – this provides structure and security.
- Outline the aim of the lesson and the way it will take shape.
- Give information in short chunks.
- Keep instructions short and clear.
- Indicate the way that the time will be divided up during the lesson.
- Provide a checklist so the student can tick off tasks as they are completed and see how many tasks are left.
- Give frequent indications of remaining time – use statements such as 'In five minutes we will move on'.
- Use a multisensory approach to keep interest levels up.
- Change the activity frequently and keep up the pace.
- Make the material as relevant as possible to real-life issues.
- Come up with innovative ways for them to record information

– can they draw it, produce a cartoon strip, fill in boxes in text, do a computer flow diagram or make a computer graphic?

- Allow the use of coloured pens, highlighters and coloured paper.
- Be flexible on occasions and respond to the mood in the classroom.

Seating

A traditional seating plan works better with students sitting in rows facing the front. This is much less distracting than having them sitting in groups facing each other (Figure 6.2).

FIGURE 6.2 SEATING ARRANGEMENTS

- Students with ADHD should ideally sit at the front of the class or at the end of a row where you can walk past.
- It is important to be able to have clear eye contact.
- Let the student keep the same position for a term if it works well. This gives stability.
- They should sit away from distractions such as a window, door, noisy pipes, wall displays or the class gerbil!
- Sit them beside a sensible 'buddy' or a good role model.
- Find an area, perhaps a computer station or a more secluded corner, where the student could go if they need a change.

Discipline

- Be very clear with the whole class about expected norms of behaviour, both commendable and unacceptable.
- Outline exactly what is not acceptable and any consequences for misdemeanours.
- Be consistent about your class rules.
- Develop a signal to attract the student's attention if it has wandered; this can be more subtle and less embarrassing than using their name.
- Signal clearly if you feel that their behaviour is becoming unacceptable.
- Give them one warning and remind them of the consequences.
- If unacceptable behaviour continues, act quickly, decisively and confidently to discipline the student.
- Do not lose your temper; try to remain calm and emotionally equable.
- Choose sensible punishments for misdemeanours, ones that you can actually carry out and that ideally 'fit the crime' as these are easier to relate to.
- Try to avoid direct confrontational arguments with the student, especially in front of the class.
- Agree to have a signal to let you know if the student is becoming too stressed, anxious or angry. A coloured card which they can put on the desk can work well with yellow and red showing mounting anxiety.
- Can you change their activity or position in the classroom, send them on an errand or give them a task in the room? Can they go to a quiet area in the classroom?
- If you feel that it is best if they leave the lesson, is there a designated place elsewhere in the school that they can go to relax and calm down? They will probably need to be accompanied.
- Try not to bear a grudge, even if the student has been rude to you. Deal with discipline calmly and firmly but try not to take it

personally. It is part of their condition and they cannot always help it.

Allowing movement during the lesson

Some students will have a constant need to fiddle or jiggle. It is an idea sometimes to let them have a stress ball or piece of fabric to fiddle with. This can aid concentration.

Try to factor in a time when the whole class can leave their seats and move around – for example, doing group work, acting out a scenario, having a debate, carrying out a practical exercise or going to look at a demonstration.

Try to allow a hyperactive student with ADHD to move periodically. Could they give out textbooks or paper or give back homework? They are likely to volunteer if you need an assistant for a task, but you have to try to balance the needs of others in the class too.

Use of computers

Interactive teaching and revision programmes are often very popular, especially if they are colourful and fun. They can give instant, non-judgemental and personal feedback, which is excellent for students with ADHD.

There is a range of quiz games and websites for producing games such as bingo that can be made to be subject-based, which students with ADHD might thoroughly enjoy playing.

Students are able to organise written work better using a word processor, as paragraphs can be moved and words adjusted without making the presentation untidy. A piece of work can then be produced and illustrated to a high standard. This can be shown to the class using audio visual equipment, which is good for self-esteem. Work done on computers can be emailed to the teacher and is less likely to get lost.

Team/pair work

- This is easiest if you choose the groups or pairs.
- Give specific roles to everyone in the groups as this avoids conflict.
- Divide the task into a series of small, achievable goals.
- Give a clear timescale to work to and remind the students, at an appropriate moment, how long they have left.
- Students with ADHD may have great ideas, but make sure their projects are realistic and achievable.
- Watch carefully for arguments or bullying.

Positive feedback, celebrating success

- Try to look out for good behaviour or work to celebrate during the lessons.
- Give immediate praise.
- Reward in a tangible way, such as a giving a sticker or house point, depending on the school system. Be consistent though, and remember that there are others in the class.
- Acknowledge improvement and effort.
- Let the student's mentor know about any successes so that they can give praise and positive feedback to the student and pass on this information to the child's parents. Often we only remember to pass on negative information, and these students need a morale boost.

Manage change carefully

Students with ADHD dislike changes in routine as this throws them into chaos. If you know that there will be a disruption in your class such as a visitor, cover teacher or a fire drill, try to let the class know beforehand. This will take away the surprise element and the student is less likely to overreact.

Responsibility in class

Students with ADHD may lack confidence and this can sometimes be helped by giving them a role of responsibility. Could there be a responsible role in some of your lessons? Is there a club attached to your subject that the student can help with?

Organisational skills (see Chapter 12)

This is an area where students with ADHD will need continued support throughout school as they struggle with planning and meeting deadlines. Individual guidance will be needed to help them develop coping strategies.

Homework

- Be aware that a piece of work will take a student with ADHD longer than the average student by the time they have settled down and then been distracted a few times. Their families may sometimes struggle all evening to keep them on target. So decide which parts are essential and which are optional.
- Give clear instructions, spoken as well as written.
- Make sure the homework is written down correctly or recorded electronically.
- Make some homework fun and different. Remember that students with ADHD love the 'fun factor'.

Marking

- Decide which things are important for a particular piece of work and mark accordingly. If it is for creative writing, mark for content and try not to worry too much about handwriting or spelling.
- Try to give positive comments.
- Give constructive suggestions for improvement next time.
- Be aware of effort and progress.

OUTSIDE THE CLASSROOM

It is helpful to understand what happens to the student before and after your lesson. Sometimes it can explain a lot about a student's behaviour.

Lunch and break times

These unsupervised times can be difficult for students with ADHD as they often find unstructured social situations challenging. They may find it hard to play informally with others, and arguments and fights can occur. The student could be the butt of jokes or may be provoked by others. Staff on duty should be on the lookout for bullying behaviour.

Strategies:

- Encourage companionship of a sensible 'buddy' to do a joint activity.
- Encourage them to attend a club or society, or sports practice, a music or art session at these times.
- Suggest they help with younger pupils' activities.

Games lessons

Students with ADHD may have excess energy to burn off. Regular sport and exercise can be an excellent channel for this and should be encouraged.

Fast action sports such as football can be very popular, especially with adult supervision to ensure that rules are observed. Informal, playground 'kick-about sessions' can end in conflict. Some team sports, such as cricket, are less suitable as they require sustained concentration, especially when fielding.

Solo sports such as swimming, running, tennis, judo and taekwondo have been shown to be to be very successful for students with ADHD. If possible, these should be encouraged. Taking a sport to a high level can offer challenges and rewards and encourages a disciplined attitude to training. Competing is stimulating and winning gives an instant reward of success.

Some students benefit from a short extra sports session before the start of school.

A VIEW FROM THE INSIDE

When most people get angry they can choose whether they explode – go into a dark tunnel – or flick the points, change direction and find another way to go. For me the tracks go straight into the tunnel – there are no diversions. It's dark; it's black and bad things happen.

After meltdown I feel really upset because I didn't want anything bad to happen but there was nothing I could do to stop it.

Taken from Daniel's story in The Boy from Hell: Life with a Child with ADHD *with kind permission from the author, Alison Thompson*

Exams (see Chapter 13)

Students with ADHD may need special arrangements for exams, including regular rest breaks. It may be appropriate to have a separate room away from other distractions, which also allows a student to move around in order to help concentration. Provision will depend on the student's needs. The SENCO and exams officer will put this in place. The student should be allowed to practise with these arrangements in school exams.

WHOLE-SCHOOL APPROACH

All teachers and staff should be aware of any students with ADHD and make sure that they know who to contact about their welfare.

The *SENCO (special educational needs coordinator)* should coordinate their care.

An *adult mentor* (a tutor or year head) supports both a student with ADHD on a day-to-day basis and their teachers.

Teaching assistants may be able to help in some lessons, which can be very beneficial to a student with ADHD, their teacher and the others in the class.

Make sure that you are also clear about the school policy and procedures. Find out about the following.

Work matters

- Does the student have any other learning difficulties?
- Do they qualify for extra time or rest breaks in tests and exams?
- Can they use a computer for assignments and exams rather than having to handwrite?
- Are there any special arrangements regarding homework?
- Do they have individual learning support lessons?

Medical matters

- Are they taking medication and how might this affect them?
- Does the medication last all day? Some older students may take it selectively so that it is most effective for the lessons requiring greatest concentration.

Behavioural difficulties

- Who should be contacted if there is an outburst?
- Is there a specified place that the student could go to if they have to leave your lesson?
- Is there a colleague in a nearby room who can help you either with the student or the rest of the class if the student becomes disruptive or violent?
- What is the school's policy on restraint?

Social matters

- How often do they report to their mentor?
- How can you contact the mentor to learn more or to pass on information?
- If the student is being bullied in any way, what is the school policy on bullying?

Consistency across all staff about excepted norms of behaviour is important and will make it much easier for students and staff to work together.

Personal, social and health education (PSHE)

PSHE lessons can be valuable times to discuss issues, for example:

- embracing individual differences
- tolerance
- anger management – some role-play might be helpful
- friendship, kindness
- body language, social communication
- bullying
- depression.

These lessons may offer an opportunity not only to tell the individual class about ADHD, and this would depend on the wishes of the student and how comfortable they are talking about it, but also to promote understanding in the wider school.

INDIVIDUAL SUPPORT

An *adult mentor* can provide a lifeline for a student with ADHD. They can meet with them regularly, help them to plan and organise their school life, and solve problems as they arise. Celebrating success and progress is another important role that a mentor can fill. Depression is common with students with ADHD and so it is important that they learn to believe in themselves, to become more happy and confident individuals.

A *learning support teacher* can provide support to the student in dealing with academic needs as they arise. Ideally they should have regular sessions.

Open communication between the student, their mentor, the subject teachers and the learning support teacher provides the most effective overall support that the student needs.

Feedback to parents

Usually this is via a named member of staff, often either the mentor or year head, and class teachers can communicate via this person. Regular feedback to parents is important, so remember to pass on your comments, good news as well as bad. It is great for parents to hear about achievements and accolades as well as areas of concern. It makes it easier for them and reinforces the idea that the teachers and parents are working together.

KEY POINTS

- -

- ADHD is a lifelong medical condition affecting behaviour. It is characterised by inattention, hyperactivity and impulsiveness.
- ADHD affects around 5 per cent of the population.
- Hyperactive/impulsive ADHD is more commonly diagnosed in boys; inattentive ADHD is seen more commonly in girls.
- Teaching style needs to be dynamic and multisensory, with frequent changes of activity to engage students with ADHD since they have a short attention span.
- Students with ADHD will need help with organisation and planning.
- Work should be set as short, manageable tasks.
- Teachers should have a consistent approach with clear classroom discipline.
- Students with ADHD are most successful when there is a whole-school policy on support and discipline and if there is a designated adult mentor.

- Students with ADHD find school tiring and often difficult, but good teacher support and a positive relationship with parents can make a huge difference.

- -

CHAPTER 7

Autism Spectrum Disorder (ASD)

★ What is ASD?

★ How is ASD diagnosed?

★ What is Asperger syndrome?

★ How can I spot a student with ASD

★ Common strengths

★ Common indicators (downsides)

★ ASD girls

★ Overall approach

★ Classroom strategies

★ Outside the classroom

★ Whole-school approach

★ Individual support

★ Key points

WHAT IS ASD?

Autism is a lifelong neurological (brain-wiring) condition. Autistic people experience difficulties with communication and social interaction, and show restricted/repetitive behaviours. They often have special interests or collections. Autistic students are likely to have sensory issues, and are either over-sensitive or under-sensitive to certain stimuli. ASD occurs over a wide range of intellectual ability and affects 1 to 2 per cent of the population. It has been more commonly diagnosed in boys, but increasing numbers of girls are now being identified.

HOW IS ASD DIAGNOSED?

ASD is a medically diagnosed condition and would usually be carried out by a community paediatrician, or a child psychiatrist. The diagnosis is based on two areas of impairment (American Psychiatric Association 2013):

- social communication and interaction
- restricted, repetitive patterns of behaviour, interests or activities.

There are 3 levels of ASD diagnosis depending on the level of support a child requires:

- Level 1 requiring some support
- Level 2 requiring substantial support
- Level 3 requiring very substantial support.

ASD varies along a continuum from a Level 1 diagnosis where students are able attend mainstream school and, if they receive the correct support, can achieve well especially in their chosen subjects.

Students with Level 2 or 3 diagnoses will need considerably more support and may have marked speech and communication difficulties or be non-verbal. Generally they will attend special schools or day centres.

For the purposes of this chapter I will be referring to ASD Level 1 students in mainstream schools.

WHAT IS ASPERGER SYNDROME?

Until recently people on the autism spectrum who had normal intelligence and language development were identified in a separate diagnostic category called *Asperger syndrome*. Some students will still have this diagnosis but in future they will simply be diagnosed as having ASD (Level 1). The name continues to be used colloquially and in older books so you are likely to come across the term.

Another recent change is the introduction of a new term: *autistic spectrum condition* (ASC). This is because there is an increasing move to see autism as a different way of thinking and not a 'disorder'. The term ASC is less judgemental and allows celebration of the positive aspects of autism including the special talents that some autistic people possess. It can be confusing, though, as the medical term is still ASD but some schools use the term ASC.

TERM OF REFERENCE

For an autistic person, autism is increasingly seen as a defining part of their personality and not as an 'add-on disability'. I will therefore be following the guidelines from the National Autistic Society by referring to 'autistic students throughout the next two chapters and not 'students with autism'. When dealing with individual students, however, I think it is still wisest to ask them or their parents about their preferred term.

Strictly speaking ASD is not a Specific Learning Difference (SpLD) but a medical condition. I have included it because special provision should be put in place in school and teachers made aware of a student's behavioural differences and learning style preferences. Students may be eligible for special exam arrangements. Some autistic students may also have other concurrent SpLDs such as dyspraxia or ADHD, but many will not.

HOW CAN I SPOT AN ASD STUDENT?

These students may appear rather 'unusual' and socially isolated. Look for the student who speaks in a rather pedantic way, often using long and complicated words. They may have a great interest in a particular topic and love to discuss it in detail. They often prefer to talk to adults and may try to have a conversation with you during a lesson (oblivious of the needs of other students). They may have a very rigid outlook and dislike change. They prefer to work alone and may wish to go into unexpected depth on certain topics, but can appear to struggle with more basic work. They do not fit in with the crowd and often have little desire to do so.

> When I first met Sarah, a Year 7 student, she arrived at her first biology lesson early. Sat at the front and arranged her pens then she announced, 'I don't like arachnids, I have arachnophobia!'
>
> *Author*

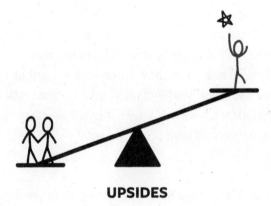

UPSIDES

COMMON STRENGTHS

- Unusual and individual.
- Makes decisions based on logic not on social expectation.
- Will not change views 'just to fit in' with the crowd.
- Likes fairness – often has a strong sense of right and wrong. Will follow rules and may try to make others do the same.
- Punctual and reliable.
- Good focus on topics of interest – likes to understand the facts fully.
- Very observant.
- Good vocabulary.
- Encyclopaedic knowledge in certain areas.
- Good at precision planning, timetables, maps.
- Can excel with electronic or mechanical devices.
- Enjoys logical subjects such as maths or science.
- May be talented in art or music.
- Creative – will often have a very different approach from others.
- Loyal to friends.
- Straightforward, not deceitful or devious.
- Can have a quirky and unusual sense of humour.
- Refreshingly honest.

COMMON INDICATORS (DOWNSIDES)

DOWNSIDES

Speech

- May be monotonal and lacking inflection.
- May have a vast vocabulary.
- May use long, complex words and pedantic language.
- May make little use of peer group jargon, or use it inappropriately.
- Can talk in great detail about a topic of interest.

Conversation

- May find it difficult to have a light-hearted conversation. Might prefer a meaningful discussion to 'small talk'.
- May not know when to start or stop speaking. May interrupt, or launch into a monologue.
- May prefer adult conversation.
- May have a very literal interpretation of words and phrases.
- May not pick up on information expressed through facial expressions or body language.
- May find it difficult to understand jokes or puns.
- May not pick up implied information.
- May find people's reactions unpredictable and confusing.
- May not easily understand irony, sarcasm and metaphors.
- May find idioms confusing unless they are explained.

Social interaction

ASD students may find other people confusing and unpredictable as they find it hard to understand social norms and unwritten behaviour patterns.

A VIEW FROM THE INSIDE

Most people in social situations understand what the rules are automatically, almost by osmosis. If you have ASD you don't get the rules unless you are told what they are.

Student

Here are some of the reasons:

- difficulty reading social cues and understanding how others think
- unlikely to pick up on unspoken signals indicating whether they are intruding or welcome
- may invade personal space or keep too distant
- there can either be a lack of eye contact, which is disconcerting and results in missing facial cues, or too much eye contact, which appears intimidating
- may not know how to respond to emotion in others and may react inappropriately
- there may be difficulty understanding the expected norms of behaviour when interacting with different groups of people, such as family, peers or adults in authority. Might be too formal with peers and over-familiar with teaching staff
- socially awkward. May be the butt of jokes or bullied
- may have very different interests from peer group
- may not see the point in just following the crowd
- may have inflexible attitude and opinions. Liable to argue
- often very honest and will appear to 'tell tales' which can land others in trouble
- may give an honest opinion, which is not always welcome. Has not learned the art of tact to avoid hurting people's feelings
- can unintentionally cause offence.

Stimming

- May show repetitive movements such as hand flapping if stressed.

THEORY OF MIND

Most children by the age of around five can read social cues so they can understand the thoughts, feelings and intentions of other people and they can predict what people will do next. The psychological term for this is *theory of mind*. This skill allows them to develop empathy with others and to see things from a different point of view. Autistic people have great difficulty reading social cues and understanding how others think, and so they can find social situations confusing and tiring.

Order and routine

Generally an ASD student:

- likes routines, timetables and order
- will have personal routines, following the same route to a classroom and likes to sit in the same place; familiarity and routine provide security and reduce stress
- dislikes change and unpredictability – can be very upset by a sudden alteration
- arranges items in an exact or particular way, such as coloured pens in a wallet, and will be disproportionally upset if this is altered
- will be unhappy about sharing personal items
- finds 'busy places' such as corridors or changing rooms stressful
- may have certain repetitive behaviour patterns or movements
- may have unusual and repeated body movements (tics), such as

arm flapping or rocking which can become more pronounced in stressful situations.

Special interest topic

Often an ASD student:

- has a special interest, which is often something in a narrow field
- will research their interest topic keenly and can be exceptionally knowledgeable about it
- may change their special interest topics as they mature
- will talk excessively about a special interest to the point of boring other people
- likes spending time doing their special interest as it is ordered, relaxing and secure

---

A VIEW FROM THE INSIDE

You have very specific interests. Things you really enjoy. They are comforting. It is sometimes easier to talk to adults about them than other children who aren't interested like you are.

Student

- has collections of items which are important. These can be unusual objects such as batteries and keys, or more generally accepted collectables such as model trains or fossils. It can provide comfort to go through the collection, putting the familiar objects in order.

Coordination

Not all ASD students have coordination problems but many do. They may have:

- an unusual walking gait
- motor coordination difficulties (similar to those seen in dyspraxia)
- gross motor skill difficulties – balancing, catching a ball, riding a bicycle
- handwriting and fine motor skills difficulties.

Sensitivity (see Chapter 9)

ASD students can be either unusually over-sensitive (hypersensitive) or under-sensitive (hyposensitive) to certain stimuli (light, sound, smell, taste, touch). This can greatly affect their lives and ability to learn in certain situations. Teachers of autistic students should be aware of any sensitivity issues and endeavour to enable the student to work around them appropriately.

Working with others

Working with others is not easy for ASD students. This is due to a combination of poor social skills and an inflexible attitude. An ASD student is likely to:

- get set on a particular idea or approach and find it hard to compromise
- feel strongly that their ideas are correct
- wish to be in charge and become bossy or appear arrogant
- have difficulty seeing another person's point of view
- find it hard to predict other people's reactions
- have problems sharing resources
- find group situations tiring so may feel a need for quiet time on their own.

Temper

Frustration, a sense of unfairness, sensory overload, tiredness or the irrationality of others can lead to strong temper outbursts. Strategies should be put in place, within school, to deal with a situation if it arises.

Masking

Some autistic students will try hard to hide many of their autistic traits in order to fit in better with their peers and to avoid being teased and appearing to be different. This can be extremely tiring and stressful. Sometimes students will 'hold it together' and mask during the school day but then have an emotional outburst (meltdown) when they are home again. Masking is especially prevalent in girls.

Depression

Depression can be a problem for intelligent students with ASD. They are aware that they are different but attempts to fit in socially or to make friends are often rebuffed. Friends are valued in the teenage years, and social rejection can lead to increased isolation and unhappiness.

AUTISTIC GIRLS

Until recently autism was a condition mainly diagnosed in boys, typically 1:4 girls to boys, and girls tend to be diagnosed two to three years later than boys. This situation is now changing and autistic girls and women are being increasingly diagnosed and understood.

Why are girls diagnosed less often?

Autistic girls are more likely to try to fit in socially than boys of a similar age. Girls may mask their autistic traits, and are therefore less likely to stand out in a class as behaving differently. Girls may mimic their peers' behaviour and adopt their mannerisms, dress, hairstyles, and even try to share interests in order to be accepted. They may try hard to have conversations and use the 'right' jargon to fit their peer group, even though the nuances of social interactions may be missed or misinterpreted. Maintaining this pretence is extremely tiring and can cause stress and anxiety which accumulates during the day. Autistic girls may also be socially immature and vulnerable. They can be the butt of jokes.

A VIEW FROM THE INSIDE

When I appear to be non-verbal, please just work with me. It is an exterior method of showing sensory overload and emotional burnout. I promise I'm not trying to be rude but I cannot express myself without causing myself further agitation.

Message from a student to her teachers

CASE STUDY: ASD

Carol was a bright, articulate girl at a top academic girls' school. She enjoyed science and maths; she wanted to be a surgeon.

Carol was autistic.

Despite scoring well in most subjects Carol struggled with interpreting open questions, especially in English language and literature, and she found creative writing particularly difficult. She could never think of enough to say and felt that she had 'answered the question' in a couple of paragraphs. Her marks were very low and since she was a perfectionist she became despondent.

She was helped enormously when her learning support teacher suggested that she include detail from each of her five senses to enhance her descriptive writing...

'What did you see/hear/feel? Was it cold or hot? Even maybe consider your intuition?' This was something tangible that Carol could apply and she made a table so that she remembered to cover each sense to enhance any of her descriptions.

This was a rule that she was happy to apply, and while her writing was perhaps still a little stilted she could embellish it and she scored much higher marks by applying this concrete framework. She passed her GCSE and happily went on to do science at Advanced level.

Takeaway idea: *Try to give ASD students a structure or procedure to follow. Support may also be needed to interpret open questions.*

OVERALL APPROACH

Autistic students can be fun to teach as they bring a different dimension to lessons and a lot of additional insight. They certainly keep you on your toes and will be quick to tell you if you have forgotten something or made a mistake! The best approach is to be *very clear and direct* with your speech and instructions.

- Be fair, firm and consistent.
- Be aware of particular sensory issues.
- Show that you value their intellect and contribution.
- Help them to find effective ways of working.
- Have an agreed signal and 'escape' if they get too stressed.

CLASSROOM STRATEGIES

Your own behaviour

- Try to behave in a consistent manner each lesson.
- Avoid indirect or rambling speech; make points clearly.
- Use short, clear sentences.
- Understand that facial expressions and body language are unlikely to be registered.
- Do not use sarcasm, and remember that humour or irony in your tone will be missed and jokes may not be understood.
- Your words could be taken literally so a phrase such as 'Return to your desk and do not move' could cause great confusion if they are supposed to be doing a writing exercise.

- Avoid idioms such as 'pull your socks up'. ASD students are likely to interpret them literally.
- Give warning of a known change such as having to move classrooms next lesson. ASD students like to have prior warning of change.
- Do not take remarks personally or assume rudeness. Autistic students may not see the point of doing something and tell you so, they may remind you of an omission or tell you that you are wrong. Remember that they are probably just being honest. Failing to make eye contact can also be misinterpreted as rude or shifty, but it could just be limiting sensory input.

Order and routine in the classroom

- Have a clear classroom routine. Do the students wait outside the room until you let them in? Do they wait until you tell them to sit down? Where are bags placed? Do you take a register?
- Have a formal start to your lessons and always begin the same way. This provides structure and tightens discipline, making ASD students feel more secure.
- If possible, allow the student to sit in the same place. The end of a row is usually preferred, as this is less hemmed in by others.
- Explain the aims and outline of the lesson and timings of activities.
- Keep the room neat and orderly.
- Ensure that books are organised on shelves and equipment is in an appropriately labelled drawer or cupboard. It will not be appreciated if the scissors are in the drawer marked glue!

Setting work

- Give very clear instructions, preferably written. Do not assume anything: include page references, question numbers, exactly what you are expecting them to do, how to lay out the work, if you want it handed in and when it should be finished by.

- Tell them when to start if it is a class exercise.
- Give time updates – 'There are five more minutes for this.'
- On occasion, try to give an opportunity for the student to do something about their special interest. They will enjoy this and it could be a chance for them to shine.

A VIEW FROM THE INSIDE

Luke Jackson was only 13 years old when he wrote *Freaks, Geeks and Asperger Syndrome* (2002) in which he gives an amusing but insightful view of school life with ASD. Here are two of his pleas to teachers:

> Teachers and support assistants please tell the Asperger kids *exactly* what they are expected to get on with.

> The key to helping a child on the autism spectrum is to always make sure you tell them very clearly what is going on, I really cannot stress this enough.

Sensitivity (see Chapter 9)

Be aware that some students may be hypersensitive to certain stimuli or hyposensitive. The stimuli to consider will be light, noise levels, chemicals in taste and smell, touch of certain materials and the pressure of touch. Make yourself aware of any aversions and try to enable the student to avoid painful over-stimulation. If they are under-sensitive find ways to help them to engage.

Heightened sensitivity can mean that ASD students can be distracted by things that others wouldn't notice, such as a crack in the plaster or a ladybird on the window frame. Exciting classroom displays and posters can make it very hard for them to focus on the lesson.

Social integration

Some social skills can be learned by patient reminders and a consistent approach. In your lessons, reinforce expected norms of behaviour and try to encourage the sharing of ideas. Encourage all students to listen to each other's ideas.

Having a short fuse

- Try to avoid a student temper flare up or meltdown if possible by managing their environment in advance and good communication with them about their (e.g. sensory) needs.
- Be aware of signs of stress and unhappiness.
- Anger and meltdowns can be the result of an earlier incident at home or school, so a student might arrive at your lesson already tense and distressed.
- It is sometimes worth having a way that students can tell you that they are feeling overwhelmed and may be getting angry without flagging it up to the rest of the class. Perhaps by holding up a coloured card.
- Look for triggers which might cause increased agitation.
- Try to anticipate or divert an emotional build-up; possibly give them a focused task to do that will relieve tension.
- Can the student leave the room on some pretext?
- Is there a classroom assistant who can help or a designated person for the student to go to?
- If they are really stressed or aggressive, let them go to the designated quiet room for a bit of 'time out'. Make sure that they know who to report to and remember you will have to tell them when to return to lessons.
- Keep calm yourself.

Group work

Appreciate that integrating autistic students into group activities can cause friction. It works better if you:

- pick the groups yourself
- give each person a specific role as this reduces arguments
- supervise carefully.

Look out for unkindness, teasing or bullying by other team members but also check that the autistic student is not being too dictatorial within the group.

Working alone

Sometimes autistic students really enjoy the chance to do a solo piece of work. This is OK occasionally, but it should not become the norm. It works best if there are other students who would also like to work alone sometimes.

Homework

Autistic students find getting through a busy school day extremely tiring and they require some relaxed 'down time' when they get home. They may also have difficulty with the concept of doing more 'school' work at 'home' and resent it. There is an argument for reducing 'homework' where possible or allowing them to fit it in during the school day, perhaps in the lunch hour.

If you set homework:

- give out homework instructions early in the lesson
- explain the work required very clearly
- give a written copy of the homework as well as spoken instructions
- tell them how long to spend on the homework
- explain when should it be handed in and where should it be put.

Project work and essays (see Chapter 12)

Some project work will really play to the strengths of autistic students. They often enjoy research and the difficulty could be stopping them from going into too much detail and coming up with something resembling a thesis.

Certain subjects are easier for autistic students, for example mathematics, science or history, where the information is logical and ordered. They can find English literature very challenging, as they struggle to see things from other people's perspectives so they find it very difficult to answer questions such as 'What was the author thinking about?' or 'What motivated [one of the characters]?'

If English is your subject you will probably need to give very precise guidelines and work with the student to help them interpret questions and learn to answer them in sufficient depth. Ask a series of short, closed questions first, to set the background for an essay. An essay plan will be useful (see Figure 12.1 in Chapter 12).

OUTSIDE THE CLASSROOM

It is worth understanding some of the difficulties in school for autistic students. This may not be directly relevant to your subject but can influence the students' mood and behaviour.

Games lessons

Autistic students may find class games lessons really hard for the following reasons:

- poor coordination, so they find team ball sports genuinely difficult
- unlikely to be picked by others for a team, which is upsetting
- may not see the point in team games
- dislike of changing rooms and crowds
- too much sensory input – shouting, whistles, movement, physical contact, mud
- the games clothing, mouth guards, shin pads, helmets or goggles may irritate
- smells such as chlorine, changing rooms, feet or deodorant may be difficult to cope with.

Sport is undoubtedly good for health, improving coordination and generating a feeling of well-being, so it should be encouraged, but some modifications will make it easier for autistic students:

- Offset changing room issues by getting the student to arrive a little early to change (see advice on dyspraxia in Chapter 5).
- Be aware of sensitivity issues. Possibly allow a variation on uniform material if appropriate (see Chapter 9).
- The teacher should pick the teams.
- Consider alternative sports – autistic people can excel in some more individual sports, for example running, swimming, climbing, dance, cycling, fencing, martial arts, kayaking, sailing and orienteering.
- Consider giving them another role within the sports department, such as being a linesman, scorer, team photographer or a roving reporter for the school journal.

Dining room

This can be very stressful for autistic students. Dining rooms are often very crowded, and noisy, with lots of people eating and chatting in close proximity. Strong smells can also lead to sensory overload. Perhaps the mentor can try to think of strategies to help if this is a problem. Can the student eat elsewhere, maybe with a few others?

Hobbies and clubs

It is much easier for ASD students to relate to others if they share common interests; attending clubs and societies can be an excellent way to develop friendships. All the students gain from cooperating in a project that is of mutual interest and benefit.

Clubs such as chess, computer, natural history, space, history and politics can be popular. Joining the technical support crew for drama productions can also be beneficial.

The highlight of the week for one 12-year-old was to be allowed to go to the senior chess club. The older students were tolerant and genuinely impressed with his ability.

Author

WHOLE-SCHOOL APPROACH

All members of staff should know and recognise autistic students and know what to do if problems arise. Special provision may need to be in place at meal times and break times and for certain lessons, such as games or science. Ideally, in school there should be a designated adult mentor. An ASD student should meet frequently with their mentor who can support them in negotiating the challenges of school.

There should also be an agreed procedure if the student has a problem in a lesson or break time. They should know who to contact and where to go – preferably a designated quiet room or area where they can go to calm down if there has been a temper incident or just to get some quiet time.

A consistent approach by all teachers to certain norms of behaviour is required, including:

- How to address a teacher or other adults
- What happens at the beginning and end of lessons
- Expected standard of behaviour during lessons
- Expected behaviour in the dining room
- Where ASD students can go at breaks and lunch times (as these unstructured times are often the most challenging)
- Whole-school policy on bullying.

Personal, social and health education (PSHE)

It can be useful to discuss the following issues not only in the class with the ASD student, but also in PSHE classes throughout the school:

- acceptance of individual differences
- friendships
- tolerance
- bullying
- social communication
- body language
- team work.

Autistic students will undoubtedly benefit from attending these sessions, but the content may need to be explained further or reinforced on an individual basis later.

INDIVIDUAL SUPPORT

An *adult mentor* is invaluable to guide and support an autistic student. The mentor can help to interpret school expectations and act as a 'go-be-tween' to communicate with subject teachers and solve difficulties as they arise. Misunderstandings are common.

The mentor can also help to keep up the student's self-esteem by praising achievement and celebrating success. They should watch out for signs of depression, self-harm, behavioural changes or any indications that the student is being bullied. Taking a genuine interest in the student will make a big difference to their well-being.

A learning support teacher will also be able to help in the following practical ways:

- improving reading body language
- teaching implied and inferred meanings
- learning to understand expressions, metaphors and similes

- interpreting the meaning of questions
- interpreting poetry
- helping with the content of essay writing
- supporting exam preparation and revision.

Learning support teachers can reinforce work covered in the lessons and lay foundations for new topics. This is most effective when subject teachers liaise with the learning support teacher.

Exams (see Chapter 13)

Special provision may be required. The student may be able to use ICT or take the exam in a quiet room away from the distraction of others. In some cases they are allowed to have extra time or an interpreter to help them to decipher the meaning of the questions. The provision will vary and it will be the role of the school SENCO (special educational needs coordinator) to put this into place with the exams officer.

KEY POINTS

- -

- Autistic people have difficulties with communication and social interaction. There is range of impairment from Level 1 to 3. Level 1 students would be in mainstream schools.
- ASD in girls is increasingly being diagnosed. Girls are more likely to mask their symptoms and mimic others and so stand out less in class.
- Autistic students find other people's reactions confusing and social interaction tiring.
- They like routine and order and find change unsettling.
- They will interpret speech literally and not understand implied meaning.
- They may be very knowledgeable about certain topics.
- They are honest and loyal but can be rejected and bullied by others.
- Given the right support they can do well at school.

- -

Pathological Demand Avoidance (PDA)

WHAT IS PDA?

PDA is a behaviour pattern seen in a small number of people who have been diagnosed as being on the autistic spectrum. PDA was first highlighted in the 1980s but it is becoming increasingly recognised as a distinct profile of autism (American Psychiatric Association 2013). It is rooted in anxiety and is driven by a need to be in control of situations and to avoid perceived expectations.

PDA students show many of the characteristic autism indicators outlined in the previous chapter but they differ in their response to perceived demands or regulations which they try to avoid. Their avoidance strategies may initially involve social methods to try to deflect the need to carry out the demand. However, if these fail, increasing anxiety can lead to stress-driven meltdowns.

PDA children try to avoid many of the ordinary requirements of daily life thus interfering with both home and school life.

HOW IS PDA DIAGNOSED?

PDA is not currently given a separate diagnosis in either of the main diagnostic manuals (American Psychiatric Association 2013; WHO 2019) so it is referred to as a *'PDA profile within a diagnosis of ASD'*. There are no standardised diagnostic tools at the time of writing. A PDA profile is identified by a doctor, usually a paediatrician.

At present it is not recognised in the USA.

HOW CAN I SPOT A PDA STUDENT?

Look for students who regularly try to avoid following instructions and come up with excuses or reasons why they are unable to do a task. If pushed, they are likely to get anxious, become angry, panic or react with an emotional response. They are often much more sociable on the surface than most autistic children and have more eye contact, but this can be superficial. Extreme mood swings are common.

COMMON STRENGTHS

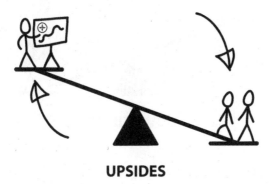

UPSIDES

N.B. The strengths will show when PDA children are relaxed and feel safe.

- Normal range of intelligence.
- Creative.
- Resilient.
- Can be good communicators.
- Good sense of humour.
- Very knowledgeable on certain interest topics.
- Often good at solving problems.
- Honest.
- Enjoy pupil-led learning.
- Like to be team leaders.
- Enjoy pretend play.
- Independent.

COMMON INDICATORS (DOWNSIDES)

DOWNSIDES

- PDA students will have a diagnosis of ASD so will show many of the traits identified in Chapter 7 but they have a different response to perceived demands.
- May appear to be more superficially sociable but lack underlying understanding.
- They may mask or hide or anxieties and try to behave normally on the outside. This can be done to a varying extent and can make the student appear to be confident and coping well.
- Students find social situations and masking tiring, and stress builds up; they can cope socially for a while but will then need time to relax in a quiet place alone.
- Like to be in control of others and dominate groups.
- May form intense relationships with peers or adults. These may become obsessive.
- Will try to avoid following instructions or expected norms.
- May find excuses or will invent reasons for not doing a task.
- May enjoy role-play, pretence and fantasy. However lines between reality and fantasy may be blurred.
- Emotional outbursts and mood swings are common.
- Avoidance of demands can vary depending on the student's tolerance to them at a particular time or their level of stress.

What things are interpreted as demands?

'Demands' can be wide ranging and are not necessarily just seen as requests imposed by others.

Different types of demands:

- *Daily life:* Necessities can be seen as 'demands,' for example getting dressed, cleaning teeth, eating meals, travelling to school, sitting in lessons, doing homework.
- *Direct requests:* Such as 'Write a paragraph about space travel', or 'Change into your PE kit.'
- *Indirect demands:* Worrying about not being in control of a forthcoming situation, time pressures, unknown places or experiences, expectations of others, even receiving praise can lead to anxiety as it suggests future high expectation and may not have the intended effect.
- *Small demands within a larger demand:* For example going on a school outing is fun for most students. For PDA students it piles on a great deal of extra stress and anxiety. They may worry about not being able to control an unknown situation, so fears such as 'Who will I sit beside on the bus? Will I be near the back and feel sick? Where are the toilets? What if I don't like the lunch? What if I get lost?' could dominate rational thought and anticipation, triggering avoidance responses.
- *Internal demands:* These include wishes such as 'things I would like to do' as well as physical needs, including drinking, eating or going to the toilet.
- *Things that are enjoyed:* These can also become 'demands' at times. They can include eating when hungry, doing hobbies, watching a favourite programme or seeing friends.

Methods used to try to avoid demands

Initially these are often social strategies, and then as pressure mounts they become more desperate and physical.

- Delay tactics – 'I'll do it tomorrow.'
- Negotiating – 'If you pick me up from school, I'll clean out the gerbil.'
- Distraction – changing the subject or diverting the conversation: 'I must tell you about...'

- Procrastination – 'I'll do it later, I'm not ready yet, I'll do it after I've finished my computer game.'
- Making excuses – 'I'm not feeling well, I have to look after my sister on Tuesdays.'
- Inventing incapacitating reasons – 'I can't come because I have a sore leg.'
- Withdrawing into role-play or fantasy characters – 'I am a tiger so I can't go to the dining room.'
- Reducing meaningful conversation – changing the subject or interrupting discussion with noises or actions to reduce it.
- Self-harm or aggression.
- Refusal.
- Agitation, tears, meltdown.
- Escaping.

Meltdowns

If the tactics described above do not work, and the student feels cornered, a rapid escalation to panic attacks can follow leading to meltdowns or running away (Figure 8.1). These are not deliberate responses, but occur as a result of mounting stress and anxiety. If the anxiety spirals to this level, students may display uncontrollable crying, destruction of property or physical harm to themselves or others, in order to 'escape'.

These responses are not deliberate or premeditated and leave the student exhausted and often depressed. It is not that they won't do something but at that moment they just can't.

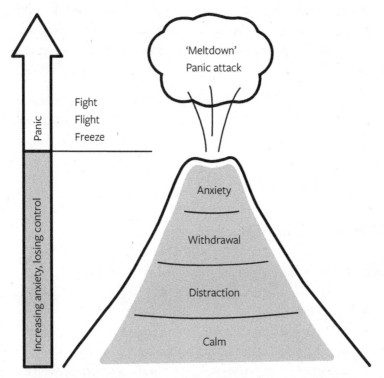

FIGURE 8.1 MOUNTING STRESS REACTIONS OF PDA STUDENT

Teachers should also be aware that for PDA students the pressure of 'demands' builds up steadily during the day. The student may even be able to mask and appear to cope while at school but will have meltdowns once they reach home and the pressure is taken off. A good analogy would be that of a shaken bottle of fizzy drink which can remain 'capped' with the top held on under increasing pressure, but as soon as the lid comes off it explodes!

A VIEW FROM THE INSIDE

For a PDA youngster to be in the right mindset to be able to learn, they need to feel that they are in control and that they have chosen the task to learn and the way in which to learn. This does not happen in a mainstream setting as work is 'forced' upon learners by the teacher. By definition, this is therefore a demand, which will be avoided. Anxiety will be raised in the learner and their need for control will be even greater. As the day goes on, this gets worse and worse until eventually a panic attack will occur.

A PDA girl aged 17 years. With kind permission from © PDA Society. This information is published in full at pdasociety.org.uk

OVERALL APPROACH

Much is about your style of approach and your demeanour.

- Try to be relaxed, friendly and adaptable.
- Talk to the student and what work together. Try to find out what they find stressful and what triggers anxiety.
- Work out coping strategies with the student and develop a way of signalling their discomfort to you before it gets too bad.
- Where possible offer alternatives rather than a single instruction which can be interpreted as a demand.
- Prioritise demands – remember, some very anxious children find it hard to get to lessons at all so decide which things are most important for your lesson and be more relaxed about some of the other 'demands'.

CLASSROOM STRATEGIES

- Discuss seating and allow the PDA student to sit where they feel less stressed – this will often be at the end of a row so they are not hemmed in and could reach the door if needed.
- Adopt a flexible attitude where possible, and be prepared to adapt an activity or allow a variety of approaches to achieve the same objective.

- Give choices where possible – 'Would you like to do the reading first or the illustration?'
- Ideally give the whole class the same choices, perhaps with the order of activities or methods of presentation, as this removes the focus from a single student.
- Re-phrase demands by choosing language carefully, instructions (demands) can then be replaced by ideas, suggestions or perceived thoughts, by using phrases such as:
  - *How about...*
  - *You might find the information you need on...*
  - *Who could help me to...*
  - *I wonder how I am going to...*
- Use humour to try to keep the atmosphere light and fun thus inviting engagement.
- Invite the students to invent board games or activities to illustrate points.
- Many PDA students will have special topics of interest. Can they be drawn into activities if an opportunity arises?
- Defuse stress – try to learn what the trigger points are and try to gauge the stress/anxiety level of your student. If you detect increasing tension, let them change the activity or take some quiet time out.
- Time out – is there somewhere quiet to go to in order to 'chill and calm down' in the presence of a trusted adult? This could be the library, the learning support department or a tutor's room.
- Have an agreed 'escape plan' if they have to leave the lesson.

With a class of 30 it is sometimes very difficult to allow a PDA student too much latitude and choice. If you have a teaching assistant helping in the lesson, this will give you greater flexibility.

Finding coping strategies

For classroom teachers, dealing with PDA students can be challenging and requires a flexible approach and a different way of thinking. Every school day is full of 'demands' and anxieties for a PDA child to overcome before they can even begin to learn and they may become increasingly exhausted and stressed. The combined role of teachers and parents is to support these vulnerable young people and help them to successfully navigate through each busy day. They can then gradually become more confident and able to find successful coping strategies enabling them to both learn, and to thrive in later life. They will not grow out of PDA, but they can learn how to live successfully with it.

WHOLE-SCHOOL APPROACH

It is important that there is an approach adopted across the whole school for PDA students and for the school to liaise with their parents. All members of staff should be aware of PDA students and what to do if a meltdown occurs. There should be an agreed person to report to and a place for the student to 'escape' to if their stress level is getting too high. It may be that the student works some of the time in the special educational needs department alongside a specialist teacher. Schools and resources vary, but a consistent approach will help enormously. Teaching assistants can provide invaluable extra help within lessons.

INDIVIDUAL SUPPORT

Most PDA students will have an Individual Education Plan (IEP) or Education and Health Care Plan (EHCP) and their progress and welfare will be monitored by the SENCO. They will most likely also have a year head or tutor who will liaise with their parents. They may have 1:1 support from a teaching assistant for some hours each week. There may be some days when the student will have to work from home as they are unable to make it in to school. A flexible approach is essential.

A word of caution

Behaviour displayed by PDA children can appear to be challenging and rebellious in a school setting. It is therefore very easy for teachers to misinterpret PDA behaviour and decide that children are being naughty and disobedient. Sometimes PDA is confused with a condition called *oppositional defiant disorder* (*ODD*), which is a psychiatric behavioural disorder where children exhibit disruptive and destructive behaviour (see Appendix 2 for a comparison table). It is vital therefore for teachers to understand what is driving any disobedience and to remember that PDA children are not being deliberately naughty but that they feel they can't do a particular task at that time, due to worry, stress and increasing anxiety.

KEY POINTS

- PDA is a trait seen in some children who are on the autistic spectrum.
- It is related to anxiety and a fear of not being in control.
- Students try to avoid perceived demands.
- They will try to use social strategies as part of the avoidance.
- Students may appear sociable but lack understanding.
- Masking real feelings is common.
- If anxiety builds up, it can lead to a meltdown.
- A flexible approach to teaching is helpful
- Avoid direct commands where possible.
- A whole-school strategy is essential.
- PDA can be misinterpreted as bad behaviour.
- Students need help to find coping strategies.

CHAPTER 9

Sensory Processing Disorder (SPD)

★ What is sensory processing?

★ What is SPD?

★ How is SPD diagnosed?

★ Common strengths

★ Common indicators (downsides)

★ Overall approach

★ Classroom strategies

★ Key points

WHAT IS SENSORY PROCESSING?

We continuously receive information through our sense organs and it is then passed to the brain for interpretation. Sight, hearing, smell, taste, touch and temperature are the well-known senses. In addition we also have a sense of balance and motion owing to information from receptors in the middle ear, and we have a sense of position and movement because of stretch receptors in the muscles, joints and tendons. Internal receptors also give us an indication of hunger, thirst, itching skin, temperature and a need to urinate or defecate.

Sensory processing is the how *the brain interprets incoming stimuli from our sense receptors* (Figure 9.1). It is *automatic and generally subconscious.* Information is integrated, and appropriate responses occur. For most people, sensory processing develops naturally during childhood. We also learn to prioritise sensory inputs and ignore some incoming information that is continuous, such as the feeling of the material of our clothes on our skin, and we are unaware of them unless something changes. For some people, however, these background stimuli cause constant irritation and discomfort. For others the stimuli need to be much greater in order to register at all.

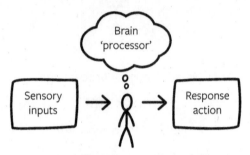

FIGURE 9.1 PROCESSING SENSORY INPUTS

WHAT IS SPD?

For some children, sensory processing does not develop efficiently and they can be either over-sensitive to certain stimuli (*hypersensitive*) or under-sensitive (*hyposensitive*). This can cause difficulties and affect daily living, learning, behaviour and social life. It is thought that 5 per cent of children (1 in 20) have sensory processing disorder when they have sensory processing difficulties with one or multiple senses. SPD often occurs concurrently with other identities such as ASD, ADHD, Tourette syndrome or dyspraxia but can also be seen in children who have no other difficulties.

SPD is more commonly seen in children, but it is thought that adults may still have it but develop coping or avoidance strategies to compensate for their difficulties.

I still shop for clothes by the feel of the material in the first instance.

Author

HOW IS SPD DIAGNOSED?

At the moment SPD is not recognised as a separate medical diagnosis but doctors can diagnose it along with another concurrent condition.

COMMON STRENGTHS

Hypersensitive

- Is aware of a greater range of sensory information.
- May take in extra detail that others miss.
- May have heightened ability to identify materials by smell or feel.
- Naturally cautious.

Hyposensitive

- Brave and adventurous.
- May appear stoical as there is a high threshold to discomfort.
- May have good voice projection.
- Can be good at certain sports. Will train hard.
- Will try new things and search for new approaches.

COMMON INDICATORS (DOWNSIDES)

Hypersensitivity

Hypersensitive students become upset and anxious when physical stimuli become too great for them (e.g. in crowds or group activities). They may try to run out of a noisy crowded place if the sensory load is too high and they feel that they can't cope. Table 9.1 shows some typical responses to sensory stimuli.

Table 9.1

STIMULUS	RESPONSE
Light	Tries to avoid strong sunlight, shades eyes, and seeks shadow. Bright classroom lights, especially if they are fluorescent, can cause distress and headaches.
Sound	Upset by loud noises. Certain pitches, often high notes, can cause great discomfort. Dislikes background buzzing of lights or electrical equipment as this intrudes and makes concentration difficult. Background conversation can be equally intrusive.
Touch	Avoids certain textures in clothes. Labels on clothes may irritate. Dislikes being touched by others even lightly. May have a low pain threshold.
Temperature	May be very sensitive to temperature and changes. May be uncomfortable in both hot and cold conditions.
Smell	Finds certain smells very unpleasant and can cause nausea. Paints, chemicals, lunch cooking, perfume.
Taste	Some flavours are too strong and unpleasant – likes bland foods, may appear to be a fussy eater, avoids certain foods and may prefer raw crunchy food to cooked food. Some textures of food are unpleasant.

Movement Posture Coordination	May be afraid of gym equipment and heights. Very cautious, avoids risk. May get travel sick or suffer from vertigo.
Internal	May complain of internal pain and tummy aches.

If teachers are aware of hypersensitive students and learn what their main problems are, they can help to minimise the students' exposure to these stimuli and therefore bypass difficult and stressful situations. Stressful situations could be:

- busy corridors at the change of lessons
- changing rooms for sport
- visiting toilet blocks
- school dining room
- assembly
- dance, sport or drama lessons
- classrooms with bright lighting
- noise and bustle in certain areas in school, especially at unstructured times such as break and lunch time
- school bus and public transport.

Hyposensitivity

Hyposensitive students need increased stimuli to respond to and often fidget a great deal to induce sensory feedback from their muscles. They are sometimes referred to as *sensory seeking*. Some students will have decreased feedback from muscles and tendons and balance receptors, and so they may have gross or fine motor coordination difficulties. They often jiggle to increase muscle awareness. They may chew gum if allowed, or suck other objects or materials, often the sleeves of clothes. They may lean on peers or jostle. They enjoy rough play and are more liable to have accidents. Table 9.2 shows some typical difficulties and responses.

Table 9.2

STIMULUS	RESPONSE
Light	Likes bright light and flashing coloured images. Enjoys interactive computer programs.
Sound	Enjoys loud music and background sound. May talk loudly and shout.
Touch	Likes a firm hard touch. May play too roughly with others. High pain threshold so may get small injuries without worrying. Likes to be tightly wrapped up in a heavy blanket to relax.
Temperature	May be less sensitive to external temperature.
Smell	Likes strong smells and will seek out certain smells.
Taste	Likes strong food flavours, such as chilli.
Movement Posture Coordination	May have poor fine motor skills for tasks such as writing. Can be rather uncoordinated and appear clumsy if muscles and movement feedback from sensors are less efficient. Can't sit still, fidgets. Seeks sensory feedback so will jump or spin and take risks. Does not easily get dizzy.
Internal	May not automatically feel hungry or thirsty so has to be reminded to drink or eat.

OVERALL APPROACH

- For the *hypersensitive* student, learn which stimuli the student is hypersensitive to and cause distress. Be alert to changes in their demeanour when they feel anxious or uncomfortable. Be sympathetic and try to find ways to avoid or reduce problem stimuli for the student.

- For the *hyposensitive* student, be aware of the student's hyposensitivity to certain stimuli and discuss with them how to increase feedback without disrupting the class.
- Let the SPD student know that you understand.
- Individual classroom teachers can help make it easier for an SPD student, but it is better when there is a whole-school approach providing coordinated support throughout the day.

CLASSROOM STRATEGIES

Hypersensitive students

Depending on the student's problem some possible strategies could be as follows. Some would need a whole-school approach.

- Try to warn the student if a loud noise is expected (e.g. the fire alarm going).
- Let them wear earmuffs when working quietly to remove background noise or listen to quiet music through headphones.
- Try to avoid classrooms or areas with powerful lighting. Is there an alternative location? Can they sit slightly away from the glare?
- Check if any materials used in games lessons, such as tabards, swimming hats or shin pads, are unpleasant to the student. Similarly are science/DT overalls or goggles causing distress? If so, is there an alternative? Cutting scratchy labels out of garments will help.
- Allow a slight variation on the official uniform if the materials irritate.
- Be aware of smells such as recent painting, cooking and chemicals in science labs. Try to keep windows open and allow the student to sit near a window or open door. Some students like to have a tissue with a known pleasant smell on to sniff.
- The student may prefer to sit at the end of a row in order to feel less 'trapped' or 'jostled' by other students.

- Individual sports could be better than group games. Swimming, dance, martial arts, cycling, kayaking. Try to find a sport for the student to enjoy and excel at.
- Can you create a quiet area in the classroom?
- Allow them to leave lessons slightly early to avoid crowded corridors.
- Look at the dining room arrangements. Is there a quiet area? Could they eat in another room with just a few others?
- Could they be excused assembly?

A VIEW FROM THE INSIDE

The reason why I enjoy having my headphones on me constantly is that it calms me down knowing that I always have a sensory regulation method to fall back on when things go wrong.

Message from a student to her teachers

Hyposensitive students

Classroom strategies will vary depending on a student's needs, but here are some suggestions:

- Allow regular movement breaks in class.
- Encourage regular changing of body position and a quick stretch of muscles.
- Introduce physical warm-ups before lessons, such as a few star jumps, hand shaking, running on the spot. This increases body awareness and blood flow.
- Let them sit at the end of a row so fidgeting and the need to get up and down will be less distracting to others.
- Allow the use of a fidget toy to squeeze and increase muscle feedback.
- Try letting them use a rubber resistance band around their

ankles or one leg and a chair leg so that the student can push against the band to get feedback.

- Address the student by name clearly before asking a question as this will click them back into listening.
- Change activities frequently.
- Talk to them and the whole class about personal space.
- Some supervised physical activity before the start of the school day or at lunch break is useful if this is possible.
- It may be that the student would benefit from seeing a physiotherapist periodically to give exercises for muscular coordination and balance (e.g. working with balance balls or wobble cushions if muscular coordination is poor).
- Be aware that games lessons can be difficult because of poor coordination and injury can occur.
- Encourage individual sports such as martial arts, swimming, athletics, gym, dance.
- Science teachers should be aware of any students who have motor coordination difficulties for safety reasons
- Check the dining room arrangements. If students have to carry full trays of food and water, it may be wise to put a buddy system in place.
- Be aware that handwriting might be affected (see Chapters 4 and 5).

Most SPD students will learn to cope with their difficulties and will develop well. Supportive teachers and schools can make their school years less stressful and happier.

School support can be greatly enhanced when there is good communication with the student's parents so worries can be relayed and extra provision put in place.

KEY POINTS

- -

- We process information from our sense organs giving us an awareness of our surroundings and the ability to react.
- We have many senses: sight, hearing, smell, taste, touch, temperature, balance, movement, body position. There are also internal sensations such as hunger, thirst or the need to urinate.
- Five per cent of children have a sensory processing disorder.
- Hypersensitive children are over-sensitive to certain stimuli.
- Hyposensitive children are under-responsive to certain stimuli.
- A sympathetic approach and simple classroom adaptations can make the lives of SPD children much happier.

- -

CHAPTER 10

Obsessive Compulsive Disorder (OCD)

★ What is OCD?

★ How is OCD diagnosed?

★ How is OCD treated?

★ How can I spot a student with OCD?

★ Common strengths

★ Common indicators (downsides)

★ Overall approach

★ Classroom strategies

★ Outside the classroom

★ Whole-school approach

★ Individual support

★ Key points

WHAT IS OCD?

OCD is a psychological condition. It is classified in a group of disorders where people experience thoughts, urges, doubts and images and they need to complete repetitive behaviours in order to obtain temporary relief. OCD affects boys and girls of school age. About 1 to 2 per cent of children are diagnosed with OCD.

OCD is thought to be related to changes in brain chemistry. A student with OCD will need considerable support and understanding at school as the condition can severely impact on school life, academic achievement and relationships.

OCD ranges in severity from mild, which may go undetected, to very severe where the student might find it almost impossible to leave the house and may need to be home educated for a while.

It is not fully understood what causes OCD but it can run in families, suggesting that there is a genetic link, but environmental factors such as illness or stressful events in a child's life can contribute to the onset of OCD.

OCD often occurs alongside other conditions such as depression, ADHD and ASD. It is sometimes these other conditions which are identified first.

It is important that teachers understand OCD and how best to help a student who has this confusing and debilitating disorder. Frequently OCD is not diagnosed for some time and it is generally not well understood.

WHERE DOES THE NAME COME FROM?

Obsessions are unwanted thoughts, images, urges and doubts that are involuntary, intrusive and irrational but they are very genuine and cause great stress and anxiety. Typically these might include severe fear of disease or visions of loved ones being killed or injured.

Compulsions are ritualistic and repetitive actions which are carried out in order to attempt to stave off the terrible fears becoming a reality. Sometimes these actions can seem bizarre such as repeating phrases or routine or avoiding cracks on the pavement, but the person feels that it is vital to perform these rituals to avoid their feared disasters from occurring.

Both obsessions and compulsions are part of the OCD condition.

The OCD cycle

Carrying out the compulsions takes time and energy and only provides temporary relief from the obsessive thoughts (Figure 10.1). The person with OCD may also try to avoid certain situations which they perceive as potentially dangerous. This can affect punctuality, performance and relationships.

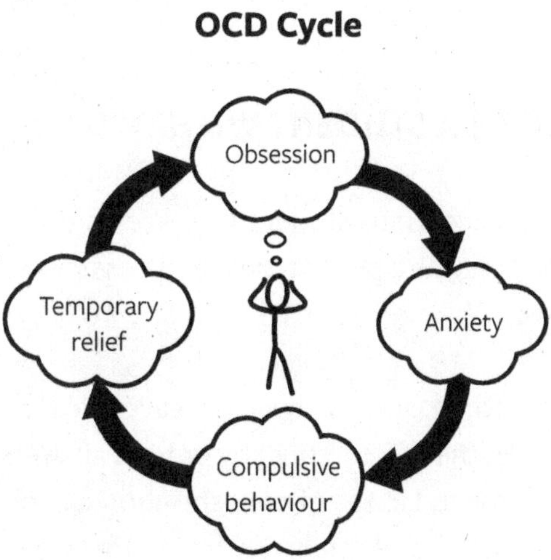

OCD Cycle

FIGURE 10.1 THE OCD CYCLE

HOW IS OCD DIAGNOSED?

OCD is frequently underdiagnosed. As it is a psychological disorder a psychiatrist specialising in children and adolescents would typically diagnose OCD in young people of school age. It is often a long process as this assessment would follow a referral from a GP.

HOW IS OCD TREATED?

The most effective long-term treatment for OCD has been shown to be cognitive behavioural therapy (CBT). This is a way of retraining the brain to think differently about obsessions and to resist doing the compulsions. It is a lengthy and tiring process but can be successful. A complete cure is unlikely, but people can learn to manage their OCD symptoms and live relatively normal lives.

Sometimes medication is also given. This is usually to increase the activity of the brain chemicals (neurotransmitters). This can reduce anxiety and allow the student to study better and feel more able to tackle CBT.

Learning relaxation techniques or yoga can also be useful for some people.

HOW CAN I SPOT A STUDENT WITH OCD?

Look out for a conscientious student who seems excessively anxious and worried. They may be a perfectionist and be very meticulous about order and tidiness.

They may be late for lessons or have to leave a lesson in a stressed state. They may visit the toilet frequently or have an aversion to sharing materials or equipment. Lapses of concentration can occur. They may show a dislike of crowds and keep away from others.

Many students are embarrassed by their OCD so they try to hide the symptoms to avoid ridicule. There is a range of different indicators depending on a student's obsessions and compulsions. Below are some of the more common characteristics.

COMMON STRENGTHS

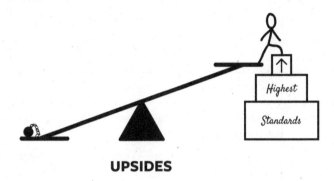

UPSIDES

As OCD affects students of all types and academic abilities it is difficult to generalise where their strengths lie. Many students, however, show some of the following qualities:

- sensitivity
- thoughtfulness and caring for others
- kindness to younger children
- orderliness and good organisation
- perfectionism – aiming high and working hard, ability to produce excellent work
- accuracy and care
- good eye for detail
- talent in art, music or sport.

COMMON INDICATORS (DOWNSIDES)

DOWNSIDES

A few of the most common obsessions and compulsions which students can show are given in Table 10.1. Symptoms vary widely so a student may show some of these indicators only.

Table 10.1

OBSESSION	COMPULSION
Contamination: an irrational fear of dirt and germs	Excessive washing – may shower several times a day, frequent hand washing. Not wanting to touch others or items touched by other people such as door knobs, keyboards. Wiping toilets with disinfectant wipes. Avoiding public toilets if possible. Refusing to share food or use communal eating utensils. Insisting on clean clothes daily. Fears of shared clothing in school, games tabards, overalls, etc.
Need for certainty: excessive worry and checking	Checking items several times (e.g. has school bag got everything?). Re-reading instructions many times. Repeating questions in class to calm worries and seek clarification.
Need for symmetry and order to avoid consequences	Arranging books, pens, equipment before beginning a task. Wanting to sit in the same place. Numbers and symmetry – dislike of uneven numbers or certain 'unlucky' numbers. Likes classroom routine, may panic if there is change.
Perfectionism	May re-write work several times. Work is crossed, rubbed out or ripped up as 'not good enough'. May hand in work late due to re-writing.

Loss: anxiety about running out of something	Hoarding items. Having numerous spares.
Fear of harm: frequently there is a fear that loved ones will be hurt or killed	Many compulsions necessitate carrying out certain rituals to avoid harm occurring to themselves or to others. Examples would be: repeating a set phrase a certain number of times, counting words on a page or bricks in a wall, touching items in a set order. Superstitious about certain numbers, colours, items, words.
Worry about hurting a friend or family member	Fear of carrying out an imagined violent act leads to worry about using equipment or substances perceived as potentially harmful (e.g. sharp instruments, strong chemicals, Bunsen burners).
Sexual or religious fears	Worry about making inappropriate sexual actions or fear of being sinful. Avoidance of social interactions.

A VIEW FROM THE INSIDE

After I had washed my hands at school I would have to nudge the tap off with my wrist, so that I did not have to touch the tap or anything else that other people may have touched with dirty hands.

From Touch and Go Joe: An Adolescent's Experience of OCD *by Joe Wells*

Triggers

Something that initiates anxiety and an obsessional thought is called a trigger. This then leads to the perceived 'need' to carry out a behaviour routine or compulsion.

It can be something as simple as sharing a pencil or touching a door knob that triggers a contamination fear. If it is not possible to carry out the compulsion to counteract the fear, it will cause great stress and even panic.

OVERALL APPROACH

Work closely with the SENCO and learn about your student's worries, behaviour patterns and triggers. Also find out about any treatments which they are undergoing, if this information is available, as this could affect learning and classroom behaviour.

Make it clear that you believe in the student and their ability, and that you are not judging them by their OCD.

Be kind and approachable and realise that they may be embarrassed by their compulsions.

Try to have a time when they can come and talk to you individually to discuss strategies that could help them.

CASE STUDY: OCD

Emma was a worrier. She was a perfectionist and often had to re-do her work several times if she made a mistake, which took hours, and she was always tired. She was intelligent and articulate and despite being praised by teachers she was rarely satisfied. She was also very worried about germs and so feared for her health if she had to share equipment in class. She tried to avoid touching people or door handles or using school toilets. She was afraid of contaminating her family with school germs so she tried to wash away all traces of school 'dirt' before she went home. She wiped the door handle of her house before entering in order to protect her family. Invasive worries about her family becoming ill could affect her throughout the day making it hard to concentrate, and she felt a compulsion to perform a tapping ritual with her hand in order to make things better whenever these thoughts occurred. The constant worry was exhausting.

Once she had been diagnosed with OCD things began to improve. She was offered support and her parents, and teachers began to understand her difficulties. Her diagnosis enabled her to come to terms with her OCD and she is currently trying a course of CBT, which is helping her to deal more positively with her worries and controlling her rituals. She finds that she can concentrate better in lessons now her teachers understand and no longer expect her to share or sit too close to others. Her friends are more supportive now that she can talk about her OCD and so she is happier.

Her parents are in frequent contact with her doctor and with school and they are working together to support her. She has special exam provision in place now and her future is looking rosier.

Takeaway idea: *A sympathetic approach from school and collabora-tion with parents and doctors will give the best all-round support for students who have OCD. With support they can thrive.*

CLASSROOM STRATEGIES

- Keep calm and be consistent in your manner.
- Understand that OCD obsessions can disrupt concentration and cause internal distractions. This will slow performance and the student may appear to be inattentive and anxious at times.
- Be prepared to listen to the student and take their worries seriously. Do not belittle their anxiety but find out if there are any practical ways to help alleviate anxiety in your lessons.
- Let them know that they can come and talk to you individually at an agreed time.
- Remember that most students with OCD really want to do well.
- Keep relaxed and cheerful – a smile goes a long way.

Planning lessons

- Have a set routine for the start of lessons as this is reassuring and provides structure and security.
- Make it clear that the classroom is a safe place where you expect everyone to make mistakes as this is part of learning; this might help other students as well.
- Outline the aim of the lesson, the structure it will follow and the way that the time will be divided during the lesson.
- Give a warning a few minutes before changing activities.
- Provide a checklist so the student can tick off tasks as they are completed. This gives a secure framework.
- Have a sensitive approach to the student's fears and worries. Be aware of potential problem situations and try to avoid any triggers. For example, if they have a fear of contamination, do not expect them to share equipment or wear communal lab coats or sports bibs.
- If any group work is to be done, make sure that you choose the groups or pairs carefully.

Seating

- A seating arrangement with rows can be less stressful than sitting around tables facing other students. Compulsive behaviours are also less likely to be noticed and commented on by others.
- Let the student sit at the end of a row rather than the middle as they will feel less trapped.
- If they have separate tables or desks, try to allow space around their desk if possible.
- Allow them to use the same desk each lesson.
- Leave a clear exit route to the door if they need to leave.
- Let them sit in a position where you can have eye contact. This allows you to monitor them without drawing undue attention. You can see if they become distracted or restless. They will also

be able to signal to you discreetly if anxiety is growing or they need to leave the room.

- Is there a colleague in a nearby room who could help you either with the student or the rest of the class if the student becomes very upset or their anxiety causes an outburst?

Marking

- Give positive feedback where possible.
- Be constructive with your comments.
- Do not put too much emphasis on grades.
- Reward effort and progress.
- Celebrate good work

Dealing with compulsions in lessons

- If they are relatively minor routines, you can ignore them rather than draw attention to the student, as long as they are not disruptive.
- Look out for any new unusual and repetitive behaviour patterns. These could be new compulsions. It would be worth passing the information on to the SENCO or mentor.
- Be aware of signs of stress building. Try to defuse a situation if possible – this may be enough but it could be that they will need to leave the lesson to go to the designated person and place in school.

Homework

Be aware that students with OCD may take much longer completing a piece of work than other students. This may be due to compulsive behaviour, such as having to have everything 'just right' in order to start. Alternatively, they might be dissatisfied with the work so start several times. Other unusual compulsions, such as counting every word on a page before turning over, can also severely hamper progress.

- Set small amounts of homework so that it is manageable.

- Give out written instructions for homework or classwork.
- Do not reprimand the student in class for late or incomplete homework.
- Allow more time for longer assignments to be completed and ask to see small sections over an agreed time frame.
- Allow the use of assistive technology where appropriate.
- Try to be flexible, especially if the student is undergoing CBT sessions. These can be exhausting and it may be better to abolish or greatly reduce homework at this time.

Positive feedback, celebrating success

- Praise is important for all students but especially those with OCD who suffer badly from self-doubt.
- Acknowledge effort and progress.
- If the student has a particular talent, try to find occasional opportunities to let them use this skill and shine, as this is good for their morale.
- Recognise that resisting carrying out compulsions is also a major success. If you are aware that they are doing this, a quiet word of praise would be appreciated.

Embarrassment with peers

Students are often embarrassed and do not want to lose face in front of others, so it is very important that you do not draw undue attention to them or to any unusual behaviour patterns they may have.

- Do not tease the student or mock their behaviour, even in a light-hearted way.
- Do not tolerate any teasing or negative remarks from their peers.
- If they arrive late for a lesson, let them come in quietly and without criticism. It could be that they have had to carry out a time-consuming compulsion on the way.
- Talk to the student and develop a signal that they can use if they feel the need to leave the room due to a build-up of panic.

- Know what the procedure should be if they do leave the room. Do they go to the 'safe person' or a quiet place such as the library? It could be that spending just a few moments outside the room is enough to regain control and they can come back and continue.
- Let them leave your lesson a few moments early at the end to reduce stress caused by crowded corridors or changing rooms.

TYPICAL COMMENTS FROM STUDENTS WITH OCD

'My obsessions and compulsions really affect school. When the scary thoughts pop up in my head, it's really hard to concentrate and I get so scared. All I can think about is that I need to do my rituals as soon as possible otherwise something bad is going to happen.'

'I can't keep up with work and don't get to chill out with my friends as much because of my thoughts and rituals.'

Thanks to Dr Amita Jassi, principal clinical psychologist,
National Specialist OCD Clinic, London

Tests and exams (see Chapter 13)

OCD symptoms tend to get worse in times of stress, and so students with OCD may find exam times especially difficult. For public exams the SENCO and exams officer will take advice from the student's doctor. It could be that some special arrangements will be allowed, such as:

- extra time to alleviate anxiety
- rest breaks if the tension build-up becomes too great
- a separate, quiet place to take exams.

For internal tests and exams the advice of the doctor and SENCO should be followed. It may be that the student should take modified papers and be separated from the other students.

OUTSIDE THE CLASSROOM

School life can be a great strain for students with OCD and they may feel worried and anxious at several points during the day. Every student with OCD is different and their triggers and anxieties will vary. The ways of helping them will also differ and a flexible approach is essential. Below are just a few suggestions.

Breaks and lunch times

These busy unstructured times can be particularly difficult, especially if the student worries about proximity to others or has anxieties about unpredictable occasions. They might be happier going to the library or having a specific role in a supervised club.

Minor timetable adjustments, such as going into lunch a little early, with a friend, can be helpful to avoid crowds. Is a packed lunch an alternative to school lunch?

Games lessons

Contact sports can be very difficult for some students. Encouraging them to help as an official, such as a scorer, linesman or photographer may be a way to involve them without them having to take part in the games.

Busy changing rooms and dirty PE kit can cause anxiety. Allowing the student to change a few minutes early or in a different place could help.

Science, design technology and cookery

Using sharp instruments, powerful chemicals or lighting ovens or Bunsen burners can be extremely worrying. If this is the case, a sympathetic approach by the teacher is important. It might be a time when a buddy system works well – if the student has a supportive partner, the jobs can be divided sensitively between them.

MORE TYPICAL COMMENTS FROM STUDENTS WITH OCD

'I always get in trouble for not listening.'

'Some other kids in my school pick on me because they notice when I am doing my rituals... I try to control it, hide it or try not to think about it – but it's really hard.'

'Some days I don't go to school at all and pretend I am sick or I get in so late because my OCD delays me in the morning.'

Thanks to Dr Amita Jassi, principal clinical psychologist, National Specialist OCD Clinic, London

INDIVIDUAL SUPPORT

Each student with OCD will need careful support and monitoring to enable them to feel valued and to reach their full potential at school.

An *adult mentor* can be vital to a student's welfare and happiness, providing stable support and giving encouragement and praise. The mentor can communicate with the student's parents and, provided that they are willing, can update relevant teaching staff about the treatment and severity of the OCD symptoms as these can fluctuate.

A lack of self-esteem and depression are common difficulties with OCD, and so it is important to acknowledge success and progress.

A *learning support teacher* can help a student to devise coping strategies to keep up with work and get through the school day. The student can then feel valued and supported in their battle with OCD.

Sensitive and supportive teachers can make a big difference in the life of a student who is battling with OCD.

WHOLE-SCHOOL APPROACH

Psychological problems are often not as openly discussed as physical problems, and the family or student themselves may be reluctant to share the information with the school. There are confidentiality issues and the wishes of the individual and family come first.

However, it is much easier for the school to be supportive if there is an open dialogue with the student, their parents and the doctor. If the learning difference has been formally diagnosed and a student and family are happy that the school is involved, it is much more effective to work together as a partnership.

It is important not to embarrass the student in front of peers, and a supportive framework should be put in place to help them feel secure and safe.

Uniformity across all staff about expected norms of behaviour is important and will make it much easier for both the student and the staff to work together. Ideally in school, there should be:

- a designated safe person (mentor) who meets the student regularly
- a way for the student to contact their mentor if a problem arises during the day
- a designated quiet place for the student to go to if they need to during the day
- a clear procedure to inform the school office or mentor if there has been a problem
- close cooperation between the school and with the student's parents and doctor so the school can be alerted to any changes in treatment

- confidentiality – respecting the wishes of the student and family
- staff awareness of the possibility of bullying and zero tolerance of it.

Work matters

All teachers and teaching assistants should know:

- Does the student have any other learning difficulties?
- Do they qualify for extra time or rest breaks in tests and exams?
- Can they use a word processor for assignments and exams rather than having to handwrite?
- Are there any special arrangements regarding homework?
- Do they have individual learning support lessons?
- Who should be contacted if the student has to leave a lesson due to stress or a panic attack?
- Is there a specified place that the student could go to if they have to leave a lesson?
- Is there a colleague in a nearby room who could help you either with the student or the rest of the class if the student becomes very upset or their anxiety causes an outburst?

Medical matters

Where possible, teachers should be aware of a student's current medical treatment as this may affect classroom behaviour and level of tiredness. This will depend on the family and student being happy to share medical information.

Personal, social and health education (PSHE)

It can be very useful to discuss with whole classes across the school a variety of issues that will apply to many students, but will be especially pertinent to those with OCD and other psychological difficulties:

- embracing individual differences
- friendship
- tolerance
- bullying

- anxiety
- depression
- relaxation techniques
- who to talk to in school about worries – the support offered by school
- who is there to give advice and help outside school – doctors, therapists, psychologists
- mental health issues.

KEY POINTS

- -

- OCD is a psychological condition in which a person experiences recurrent upsetting thoughts and repeats certain repetitive behaviours.
- Obsessions are irrational fears that occur spontaneously and are unpleasant or frightening for the student.
- Compulsions are rituals that the individual feels they have to perform in order to stop the fear from happening.
- OCD affects 1–2 per cent of the school-age population and occurs equally in girls and boys. The severity can vary.
- Students with severe OCD will find school life, work and friendships very difficult to manage.
- Many OCD sufferers will try to keep it secret.
- If OCD is diagnosed, the school needs to work in tandem with the student's parents and doctors to maintain the correct level of support.
- OCD can be managed and largely overcome with therapy and medical support.
- Supportive teachers who understand the condition can make a huge difference to the life and success of students struggling with OCD.

- -

CHAPTER 11

Tics and Tourette Syndrome

★ What are tics?

★ What is Tourette syndrome (TS)?

★ How is Tourette syndrome diagnosed?

★ Common strengths

★ Can Tourette syndrome be cured?

★ What makes it worse?

★ Overall approach

★ Classroom Strategies

★ Whole-school approach

★ Key points

WHAT ARE TICS?

Tics are repetitive, uncontrolled, involuntary movements of the body or sounds that are made (Figure 11.1).

These involuntary movements are caused by neurological (brain) differences in the areas controlling movement or speech. Some tics are simple actions, while others can be more complex.

Tics can change over time, often coming and going through a person's life. This is called *waxing and waning*. Many adults report that their tics lessen into adulthood but can still become problematic in stressful situations.

Internal tics

Tics can also occur internally such as tensing of the abdominal muscles or stomach muscles. These can be uncomfortable or painful.

Premonitory sensations

Some people get an urge before a tic which can be compared to the feeling that you get before needing to sneeze. These feelings are only relieved by carrying out the tic.

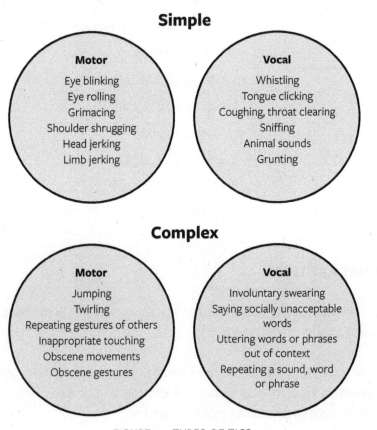

Simple

Motor
Eye blinking
Eye rolling
Grimacing
Shoulder shrugging
Head jerking
Limb jerking

Vocal
Whistling
Tongue clicking
Coughing, throat clearing
Sniffing
Animal sounds
Grunting

Complex

Motor
Jumping
Twirling
Repeating gestures of others
Inappropriate touching
Obscene movements
Obscene gestures

Vocal
Involuntary swearing
Saying socially unacceptable words
Uttering words or phrases out of context
Repeating a sound, word or phrase

FIGURE 11.1 TYPES OF TICS

Feelings include a burning feeling in the eyes before blinking, a dry throat before grunting and an itchy muscle before jerking. Some report that their skin over their whole body is itching or that their blood feels as if it is running hot.

For others, the tics occur without warning.

WHAT IS TOURETTE SYNDROME (TS)?

Tourette syndrome is also known as Tourettes or TS. It is a condition where there is a combination of vocal and motor tics which have occurred for more than 12 months.

WHERE DOES THE NAME COME FROM?

Tourettes or Tourette syndrome is named after the French neurologist Georges Gilles de la Tourette, who first described this disorder in 1885.

Children are born with Tourette syndrome but it is not usually spotted until they are around five to six years of age. About 1 in 100 children are affected, with greater numbers of boys being diagnosed. It often runs in families.

HOW IS TOURETTE SYNDROME DIAGNOSED?

For TS to be diagnosed by a doctor, tics must have been present for at least 12 months and they should include both movement and vocal tics. There is no single test for TS.

As TS can sometimes be confused with other conditions, such as epilepsy, a specialist neurologist may carry out an MRI (magnetic resonance imaging) scan to eliminate other causes.

Involuntary swearing or shouting obscenities is often the characteristic that people associate with TS but it is comparatively rare, only affecting about 10–20 per cent of people with Tourettes. This is called *coprolalia*.

Similarly, in a minority of cases, there can be inappropriate gestures or touching. This is called *copropraxia*.

Co-occurring conditions

It is estimated that approximately 85–90 per cent of children with TS have co-occurring conditions such as ADHD, OCD, anxiety, sleep problems or sensory processing difficulties (SPD). For some children, these conditions add greatly to their problems in school.

COMMON STRENGTHS

- Normal range of intelligence.
- Wish to succeed.
- Resilience.
- Perseverance.
- Humour.
- Creativity.

CAN TOURETTE SYNDROME BE CURED?

There is no miracle cure for TS but for some people the number and severity of tics declines towards adulthood. Tics often change over time. Even if tics do not subside totally, people who have TS can learn to live happy and successful lives.

Suppressing tics

Older children may be able to learn how to suppress or control tics and make them less obvious. They can sometimes do this for a while but it is very tiring and requires a great deal of effort and concentration. Imagine trying to stop, sneezing or scratching an itch. It is really difficult to think of anything else while doing this, and concentrating fully on a lesson is almost impossible. There can be a gradual build-up of pressure when tics are suppressed, and eventually they have to be expressed. Sometimes children become better at suppressing tics when they are at school, but when they get home they will have a need to tic excessively.

A VIEW FROM THE INSIDE

Tourette syndrome posed many barriers to learning throughout my school years. I spent so much time, focus and energy on suppressing my tics to 'fit in' that I lost out on the enjoyment of school, my energy was low, my memory was poor, and I didn't feel I could be myself.

Ione Georgakis, CAMHS Occupational Therapist and Lead Advocate for Tourette Action

Habit reversal therapy

Some children can be taught to replace one tic action with a different movement or sound/word. For example, an obscene word can sometimes be replaced with a different one, or a gesture can be modified. This can take a lot of effort and is not always possible.

Exposure with response prevention (ERP)

This involves learning ways to endure the feelings prior to tics until they subside without the tic being performed.

Comprehensive behaviour intervention for tics (CBIT)

This is a more wide-ranging treatment and is carried out by a specialist therapist. It includes a combination of relaxation techniques, understanding and avoiding triggers, and habit reversal therapy.

Medication

Medication may be prescribed but often as a last resort. Often it will be given to help with the 'package' of co-occurring conditions. It can take some time to find the right medication and dose.

WHAT MAKES TICS WORSE?

- Stress and pressure.
- Worry.
- Tiredness.
- Busy places and a feeling of being hemmed in.
- Embarrassment.
- Drawing attention to a student's tics.
- Telling students to stop or suppress tics.
- Hunger.
- Having to sit still for a long time.

CASE STUDY: TOURETTE SYNDROME

Ahmed changed schools having been bullied, and came into a new school at the age of 12. He was very talented in music and good academically. He was a sociable boy with a good sense of fun and he enjoyed sport.

In class, teachers and other students noticed some strange repeated mannerisms or tics. His teachers thought that he was being a nuisance and told him to stop. Other students imitated him at first and then started to bully him. It got more difficult when he began to make strange noises resembling a bark. At first teachers thought that Ahmed was just disruptive and he was often in trouble. Assembly was especially difficult for him as the noises seemed to get worse when the students were supposed to be silent. He became more withdrawn and the other students felt that he was different and often avoided or taunted him.

It took a year in his new school for before Ahmed was given a diagnosis of Tourette syndrome. He started to carry a special card (a Tourette syndrome passport) which outlined his motor and vocal tics. This made him feel better as he did not have to explain his tics himself. His parents asked that the class be told about Tourette syndrome, and after this his tics were largely ignored or accepted as part of his makeup.

He continued to excel in music, and when playing the piano his tics mostly disappeared. The tics got worse when he was stressed and he was given special exam provision of rest breaks and a separate room. He is much more relaxed now, and he hopes that his tics will decrease as he gets older or that he will be able to modify them, but overall he is less worried. He has friends who like him and consider his tics to be just part of his makeup. He hopes to pursue a career in music.

Takeaway idea: *Be alert to a student's mannerisms or repeated actions, they could be tics. These may disappear in time naturally, but if they remain or others occur they could be TS. Do not draw attention to them and be sympathetic and supportive.*

OVERALL APPROACH

- Be flexible, supportive and friendly in your approach and remain positive.
- Talk to the student individually to discuss seating arrangements and what would help them in class.

- Show that you understand about tics and appreciate that they cannot be controlled.
- Watch out for bullying or other students imitating tics and teasing.

CLASSROOM STRATEGY

- Do not tell a student to stop doing their tics – remember they are involuntary and they can't help it.
- Do not draw attention to tics.
- Allow the student to have a private place to tic if it would help them.
- Allow many movement breaks throughout the day, giving the student a chance to move around when needed.
- Try to help the student to be upbeat.
- Try to combat low self-esteem and give praise and encouragement where possible.
- If the student and their parents are willing, explain to the class about tics and try to clamp down on any bullying from others. Teach the class about the value of individuals and friendship.
- Arrange seating sensitively for a student with TS. Be aware of their possible tic movements. Maybe place their seat close to the door so they can leave quickly if they need to, or sit them near to the back, so attention is not drawn to them.
- Give extra time to complete tasks as tics can interfere with writing or concentration.

Reducing the build-up of stress and pressure

- Some children find a fidget toy helpful to control movement.
- Allow the student to move around frequently and if necessary to take regular breaks.
- If the student is getting very stressed and tics are more frequent, they may prefer to withdraw from the lesson to a designated calm place such as the library or medical centre.

- Sometimes tics can be suppressed with medication but this can cause drowsiness.

Exams (see Chapter 13)

- These are stressful situations which are liable to make tics worse.
- Students with TS should have their own space to feel comfortable to let tics out and not disturb others. Preferably they should be in a separate room.
- Many students with TS will qualify to have extra time in exams as tics affect speed of writing and concentration.
- If handwriting is affected, they could type exam papers or be provided with a scribe or voice-to-text software.
- They may also require rest breaks as coping with tics can be very tiring.

Tourette syndrome passport

This is passport-sized card with a name and photograph and gives information about a person's tics. It has wider uses than just at school and could be an excellent tool for a student's confidence in new and stressful situations. It can be downloaded from the Tourettes Action website.

WHOLE-SCHOOL APPROACH

It is important that all members of the school staff are aware of students who have TS and that there are clear guidelines to provide a consistent approach by all. The student's tutor or the SENCO should also liaise with the parents and create a flow of information both ways.

- Set up a regular communication channel with parents.
- Have a card system which the student can use if they feel the need to leave the room if the pressure of suppressing tics is building up.
- All members of school staff should know about the student's

TS. This should include permanent, part-time and peripatetic teachers, and pastoral, administrative and domestic staff.

- A Tourette card or A4 sheet is useful. This can give details of the student's tics and give advice to teachers which would be helpful if tics occur. The support organisation Tourettes Action has produced a downloadable sheet 'My Tic Attack Support Plan' which could be very useful.

- Extra supervision may be necessary at unstructured times such as at break or lunch to prevent teasing or bullying.

- If a student with TS is finding a lesson too stressful, there should be an agreed place for them to go to and a person to report to.

- Students with pronounced tics, especially vocal ones, could be allowed to avoid assemblies or situations where they need to sit silently.

- All teachers should be aware that a child's tics can change all the time; and if they are unsure, they should assume it is a tic.

- Teachers should understand that although tics can appear to be directed and rude, they are involuntary.

A VIEW FROM THE INSIDE

We must strive to create educational environments that enhance learning opportunities for people with Tourettes, accommodate their challenges, and harness their strengths, letting our students be their fabulous authentic selves.

Ione Georgakis CAMHS Occupational Therapist
and Lead Advocate for Tourettes Action

KEY POINTS

- Tics are involuntary and uncontrolled movements or sounds.
- For a diagnosis of Tourette syndrome (TS), movement and vocal tics must have been present for 12 months.
- Tics can change over time and some people grow out of them.
- Tics are made worse by stress, anxiety and tiredness.
- Students with tics should have special classroom and exam arrangements.
- There should be a whole-school awareness and approach.
- Students benefit when school liaises with parents and when teachers understand.

CHAPTER 12

Organisational Skills

★ What are organisational skills?

★ Why do some students with Specific Learning Differences lack organisational skills?

★ How can I spot a student lacking organisational skills?

★ Common strengths

★ Common indicators

★ Overall approach

★ Classroom strategies

★ Planning essays and projects

★ Individual help

★ Key points

WHAT ARE ORGANISATIONAL SKILLS?

The *Cambridge English Business Dictionary* (2015) defines organisational skills as 'the ability to use your time, energy and resources, in an effective way so that you achieve the things you want to achieve'.

There are three aspects to being well organised:

- *Physical:* Reducing clutter, having a tidy workspace, filing notes and books in a logical and accessible way, bringing the right books and equipment to lessons.
- *Time management:* Getting to appointments and lessons on time. Not wasting time but working effectively and then planning in time for enjoying relaxation and sport. Having good organisational skills is about making the best use of time.
- *Mental:* Thinking through priorities and planning how to fit in the required workload. Balancing work with downtime for relaxation and exercise. Making 'to-do' lists to keep on track.

WHY DO SOME STUDENTS WITH SPECIFIC LEARNING DIFFERENCES LACK ORGANISATIONAL SKILLS?

When students have *short-term memory* or *concentration difficulties*, it can contribute to a lack of organisation and a trail of lost items, missed appointments, failing to meet deadlines, getting lost and a generally chaotic lifestyle. This in turn increases stress levels and makes students flustered and unable to perform at their best.

Dyslexic students and those with dyspraxia, dyscalculia and ADHD often suffer from short-term memory problems and may therefore often seem to be muddled and disorganised. They may also struggle with the *executive function skills*, which include planning ahead and goal setting and so they often fail to meet deadlines and learn from experience.

Coupled with this, students with dyslexia or dyscalculia may also *misread written instructions* or confuse numbers and so make mistakes with times, dates, room numbers and contact details. Students with ADHD may not register instructions properly and they also have *difficulty managing time* and estimating how long tasks will take. Autistic students may have problems *interpreting the meaning of instructions* due to taking them too literally, and this can then lead to misunderstanding.

As a classroom teacher, you cannot solve all the organisational problems of every student in your care, but you can help them to cope by giving very clear instructions, dividing tasks into smaller, manageable chunks and being calm and well organised yourself.

HOW CAN I SPOT A STUDENT LACKING ORGANISATIONAL SKILLS?

These are the students who may arrive late and flustered to lessons, fail to hand in homework on time or do the wrong homework. They may forget to bring the correct equipment to lessons and miss meetings that are not part of their regular routine.

They may also stagger around carrying a very heavy book bag as they are worried about not having the right books and equipment so try to carry everything.

COMMON STRENGTHS

These will vary depending on the reason for the disorganisation and will not apply to everyone. However, I have found the majority of my disorganised students show some of the following traits:

- Often very charming.
- Friendly and outgoing, may be entertaining and amusing.
- Good verbally, may be powerful speakers.
- Passionate about subjects or causes.
- Lateral thinkers, full of interesting and exciting ideas.
- Innovative.
- Creative.
- Entrepreneurial.
- Strong at drama, music or art.
- Doggedly determined.

COMMON INDICATORS (DOWNSIDES)

Arriving at lessons

- Often arrives late and flustered.
- May forget to bring equipment, books, notes, homework.
- Frequently loses files, books and equipment.
- May have difficulty keeping files in order; papers are often muddled chronologically and between subjects.
- School bags can be too full.
- May drop books and equipment on the floor while unpacking and searching for things.
- Books may be bent, torn or muddy due to stuffing too much into a bag, dropping them or standing on them by mistake!

Short-term memory difficulties and organisation

- Cannot remember a list of items, set of instructions or a routine.
- May forget names, places, numbers and times.
- If visual memory is affected, may forget what to write down when looking down from the board so may have incorrect instructions.
- Often forgets what to do for homework.
- Does homework but forgets to hand it in or cannot remember where to put it.

Time keeping

- May have difficulty telling the time using an analogue clock.
- Often gets distracted and loses track of time.
- May fail to judge how long a task will take.
- Frequently misreads information, mistaking the time or day of an event or deadline.
- Often arrives late for appointments, or is so worried about being late, may arrive very early.

Getting to places

- Instructions or directions may be forgotten or muddled.
- Can misread times, timetables and instructions.
- Easily gets lost as may not remember a route.
- May confuse left and right – poor sense of direction.
- Often muddles names of places and people, especially if they begin with the same letter.
- Liable to go to the wrong room at the right time or to the correct room at the wrong time.

John rarely used his locker as he often couldn't find it during the first term at secondary school.

Mother of a dyspraxic teenager

Organising thoughts

- May have difficulties putting ideas into logical sequences.
- Liable to get sudden thoughts which are relevant but at a tangent to the original idea.
- May forget ideas rapidly if they are not recorded.
- May be good practically but has trouble putting ideas on paper.

Planning projects

- Can be overwhelmed by large pieces of work as they seem daunting.
- Often does not know where to start.
- May have difficulty allocating time to the different sections of a project so will spend too long on one part leaving little time for the rest of it.
- Holistic thinker so may get too many ideas very quickly covering a whole topic and not be able to compartmentalise.

- May procrastinate, putting off starting and then panicking as a deadline approaches.

OVERALL APPROACH

- Give clear instructions and deadlines.
- Try to understand the student's problems and work with them to find solutions where possible.
- Try to keep your sense of humour and a positive approach. Getting cross will only add to the student's stress level which may make them flustered and panicked, and may make matters worse.
- Be approachable and try to have a time when they can come and talk to you or work in your classroom.

Disorganised students will often opt to come and do their homework during the day in the classroom. This ensures that the work gets done and then it can be handed in immediately before it gets forgotten or lost.

CLASSROOM STRATEGY

- Have spare copies of textbooks and equipment, in your classroom. These can be lent out, saving the student stress and avoiding missed lesson time while they go back for something which they might not be able to find anyway.
- Clearly label shelves for handing in work.
- Colour-code your subject folders, textbooks and your shelf to hand books in. Stickers can be used.
- Have the shelves and cupboards in your teaching room clearly labelled with a logical system. This is especially important in a practical subject such as art, science or design technology for getting out equipment and putting it away.
- If a student is using a computer in lessons, make sure that a printer is easily accessible.

- Check that material recorded electronically can be safely stored and retrieved.
- Have a clock (preferably digital) clearly visible and use a timer to indicate how much longer there is for a particular task within the lesson. Electronic timers can be set to count down as a task progresses.

Homework

- Make sure that your instructions are very clear.
- Give out the homework early in the lesson, not right at the end.
- Try to give out written copies of homework as well as spoken instructions.
- If they have written it down, check that it is correct.
- Could they put homework or other reminders onto a mobile phone?
- Is there a school intranet where you could put the homework?
- Ideally keep to a routine about when homework is set, when it is due to be handed in and where it should be put.
- If homework can be done electronically it can be emailed to you. This is less likely to get lost.

Getting around school

Usually, in secondary schools, the teachers have set rooms and the students move from lesson to lesson. This can be very confusing if a student has a poor sense of direction.

- Clearly label your teaching room door, especially if it is in a long corridor. Colour helps here, or a picture relevant to your subject.
- If possible, check at the end of the lesson that the student knows where they are going next. This is especially important when they are new to the school or it is a new academic year and timetable.
- A buddy system may be useful to help them to get to lessons on time in the right place.

- Ideally students should have been given a simple map of the school site.

Planning essays and projects

These can seem very daunting. Holistic learners will see the magnitude of the whole task, find it overwhelming and not know where to start. More detail-oriented thinkers can end up focusing on one aspect in too much detail and not get the balance and perspective of the whole project.

It's important to give very clear instructions. The following pointers may be helpful:

- Give a clear title.
- Explain how to structure the piece of work (Figure 12.1):
  - *Introduction:* This should briefly outline the key topics to be discussed in the main body of the essay but not give any specific detail.
  - *Main body:* Each paragraph should be one point plus evidence; it should begin with a topic sentence which shows what is to follow. The rest is evidence or detail relating to that topic and follows in the next few sentences.
  - *Conclusion:* This should round off the work. It should be short and not include new ideas. This should refer back to the title. Generally the advice is to keep this short and summarise key points relating back to the title.

Planning an essay

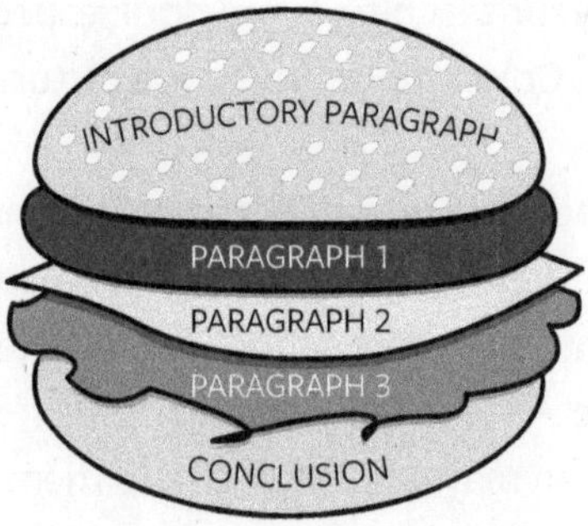

FIGURE 12.1 AN ESSAY BURGER

- Clearly indicate how long you want the essay to be. Indicate roughly the number of pages or words.
- Stress the importance of writing an essay plan before starting.
- An essay-planning frame can be a useful way to help the student to structure an essay and decide what to include in each section or paragraph (Figure 12.2).
- Emphasise the importance of relating to the title.
- Divide longer projects into smaller manageable chunks and give dates when different sections are due to be handed in.
- Be clear about when the whole project should be completed.
- How should it be handed in? Can it be emailed to you? Must it be a paper copy? Where should it be placed?

TITLE: Write out the title. Underline key words. What does the title mean?

INTRODUCTION: What are you going to talk about?

PARAGRAPH 1:

Main point:

Evidence:

How does this relate to the title?

PARAGRAPH 2:

Main point:

Evidence:

How does this relate to the title?

PARAGRAPH 3:

Main point:

Evidence:

How does this relate to the title?

CONCLUSION: What have you said? Summarise the information. Relate back to the title. Do NOT include new information.

REFERENCES: if applicable

FIGURE 12.2 PLANNING AN ESSAY

Gathering ideas

Help the student to find a way that works for them, there is no right or wrong way.

Linear thinkers may like to produce lists or bullet points with headings. These can then be arranged into the eventual paragraphs.

Lateral thinkers may find it much easier to produce a *mind map* to get their ideas written down before they are forgotten. Starting with a word or picture in the middle of the page, ideas can be assembled into different areas in 'bubbles' and detail can be added as the diagram develops (Figure 12.3).

It is possible to get advanced computer programs for mind mapping using colour and symbols to make an impact. Some programs will then change the random arrangement of the mind maps into text with a linear sequence of points.

Sport mind map

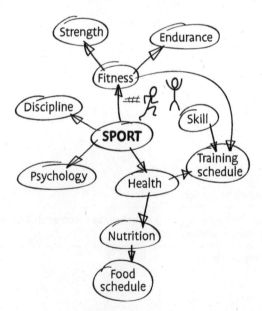

FIGURE 12.3 EXAMPLE OF A MIND MAP FOR AN ESSAY ON 'HOW TO SUCCEED IN SPORT'

Use of assistive software (see page 24)

Voice recognition software converts the spoken word into text. It helps students who struggle with writing or spelling as it allows them to concentrate on the content of what they are saying, rather than the process of writing and spelling.

Advanced spelling correction programs can also be useful. There are now some available for students with dyslexia which are based on phonetics and not on letter patterns. These are less likely to come up with wrong interpretations of the writer's intention.

INDIVIDUAL SUPPORT

Students who lack organisational skills will benefit from having an *adult mentor* to help keep them on track. Ideally they should meet regularly with the mentor and it is very helpful to invest time putting coping strategies into place to help them with organisation and planning. This support will be needed throughout school as many students come 'unstuck' when they reach the sixth form and they have more freedom.

Here are a few things that work well:

Finding things

- Label lockers and pegs with colour stickers or pictures for easy recognition.
- Make sure all books and personal items are clearly named.
- Periodically help the student to tidy a locker or desk. They will probably be in an unworkable mess.
- Colour-code different subjects' exercise books and textbooks. This can be done with stickers. These can then be easily identified.
- If work is done on file paper, students may need to be shown how to organise their work chronologically.

- Encourage the use of dividers. Files should be checked and reorganised regularly as they can rapidly become chaotic again.
- Encourage routines for putting things away.
- Make sure the student knows where to go to find lost property.

Getting to places on time

- Provide a simple plan of the school layout with lesson rooms marked.
- Make a copy of their timetable with lessons marked in different colours.
- Check that the student understands how to read the timetable.
- Mark the lesson rooms clearly on the timetable.
- Sometimes it helps to indicate how to get to the rooms, for example History Room 6 (upstairs, first left).
- Make several duplicate copies of the timetable. These can be placed in various locations where they will be seen and one spare with their mentor.
- Electronic copies of the timetable are excellent if available.
- Teach them to write down and then repeat back any arrangements, times, places, phone numbers, to make sure that they are correct.
- Instructions given electronically are helpful as they can be referred to several times as needed. Pieces of paper often get lost.

Remembering to get to special events or meetings

- If there is a school intranet it is very useful to put details of events, times, dates and places on it.
- A buddy system can work well if a friend will volunteer to remind students about meetings. It also means that they have someone to go with to avoid getting lost.
- Can the student be sent an email reminder?
- Reminders can also be set on mobile phones, if these are

allowed in school. These can be set to vibrate as a reminder of an imminent meeting.

Bringing the correct equipment and handing in homework

- Write on the timetable when PE equipment or musical instruments are needed.
- Indicate on the timetable when homework is due and where to hand it in.
- A small notebook can be handy to write reminders in if electronic aids such as phones are not allowed.
- Encourage the use of coloured sticky paper notes as reminders.
- Students will sometimes write memos into their mobile phones or record voice reminders.
- Encourage the use of 'to-do' lists. Having a small white board at home can be useful to write a 'to-do' list on. It is very satisfying wiping off or crossing out when tasks are finished.
- A weekly planner may help here in addition to the timetable (Figure 12.4).

Weekly planner

	Mon	Tues	Weds	Thurs	Fri	Sat
Bring to school	Swimming things Trumpet	Games Kit	Games Kit	Trumpet		Paper Round FOOTBALL
Hand in	English French	Maths Geography	ART	Science	History	
Special clubs / lessons	BRASS BAND		Football practice	Trumpet lesson	Football practice	
Homework	Maths Science	History	French	Geography	ENGLISH ART	
After school	Take home wet swim things	Trumpet ractice	Trumpet practice	Football club		

FIGURE 12.4 AN EXAMPLE OF A WEEKLY PLANNER

Meeting deadlines

Students with executive function difficulties do not find it easy to plan their time and think ahead. They will need to be shown how to prioritise, set targets, meet deadlines and pace themselves sensibly.

A term planner can be a very useful tool as coursework deadlines, exams, plays, sports fixtures and other important events can be written onto it. Students can then anticipate pressure points when events coincide, for example if the school play is on the week before the history coursework deadline, or a football tournament weekend is the weekend before an art exam.

There are always pressure points in any school term, but it makes it a great deal easier if these can be anticipated and planned for.

Emergency safety nets

- The mentor can arrange for spare pencil cases and maths equipment to be available in a central place in school to borrow in an emergency,
- The student should be able to contact their mentor at set times, to talk through difficulties as they arise. This should be encouraged as early intervention can prevent a crisis point occurring with conflicting deadlines and pressures.
- Sometimes the mentor will have to be a 'go-between' with other staff members if the student's workload has got out of control.
- It is sometimes sensible to 'wipe the slate clean' and start again with only essential work being tackled. The mentor and SENCO could advise here.

KEY POINTS

- -

- Neurodivergent thinkers often have problems with organisation.
- Organisational skills include time keeping, bringing the correct equipment to lessons, remembering instructions, and the executive skills of planning and goal setting. Students will have to put special effort into all these areas to succeed, and it will be tiring for them.
- Teachers can help by having spare equipment and a clear system of labelling for books and materials. It also helps if the teaching room is easily recognisable.
- Dividing large projects into small manageable chunks with regular checks helps to guide students through tasks which are seen as daunting.
- Teachers who are approachable and calm can help disorganised students enormously. If students feel that they can discuss work and time management problems with a teacher before they hit a work overload crisis, it will provide a 'safety valve' and keep them afloat.

- -

- - - - - - - - - -

CHAPTER 13

Exams and Revision

★ Common pitfalls in exams:
Mistiming revision
What to revise
How to revise
Getting exhausted
Organisation on the exam day
In the exam
After the exam

★ Special arrangements in exams

★ Key points

Exams are a stressful time for most students, but those with learning differences may find them really frightening.

These students may have a history of underperforming, and short-term memory problems, which will mean that they are unable to do the last-minute cramming that their peers may get away with. This may increase stress and then panic follows. We are all less able to think clearly when the emergency 'fight or flight' response kicks in, and this can increase the chances of errors in reading and interpreting questions.

Students can even sometimes go blank and be unable to answer even simple questions on a topic they know well.

As teachers, we can try to reduce exam pressure, where possible, and to help the students to be well prepared, so that there is less last-minute panic.

I will concentrate on the 'pitfalls' awaiting students with SpLDs.

PITFALL 1: MISTIMING REVISION

Many teenagers have problems with planning and thinking ahead (executive function tasks). This means that work is often left to the last minute and accompanying short-term memory problems mean that trying to revise the night before will not result in success.

Students should be encouraged to make a *revision timetable* in the weeks before exams. This should be based on a calendar with the days marked off and divided into blocks for different subjects. This can be done electronically if this is their preferred medium. Rest and relaxation should also be timetabled in. The days can then be crossed off and progress can be seen and a last-minute panic can be averted.

> A very articulate but disorganised student arrived at my door four hours before her GCSE Biology exam. After entering and dropping her bag on the floor she said 'Dr Hudson, please could you just go through all the biology that has eluded me over the last two years!'
>
> *Author*

It is also useful to have a large copy of the *exam timetable*, maybe displayed on a wall, so that the order of the exams can be seen at a glance. This allows priority to be given to subjects which occur first, especially if there is some free time in the middle of the exam period. It is also a joy to cross them out once the exams are over!

PITFALL 2: WHAT TO REVISE

Some students will get too bogged down and feel that they have to learn every minute detail and example. Others will have a more superficial, broad knowledge but do not have enough facts and key words in their armoury when it comes to getting marks. The art is to aim for somewhere between the two extremes.

I always advise students taking external exams to use the syllabus very closely as a guide. The syllabus outlines exactly what is expected. It will say which definitions must be known and the level of knowledge needed. It is helpful if you provide a list of revision topics to guide internal exam candidates.

Revision guides can be helpful as the student's own handwritten notes can be inaccurate or muddled. Learning the key facts and understanding concepts is the aim of revision. Exams are generally based partly on recall and partly on skills which require a clear head on the day.

PITFALL 3: HOW TO REVISE

The pitfalls here are best illustrated again by the two extremes:

- The *perfectionist student* might make beautiful 'revision notes' which are virtually the whole subject re-written. This can take hours to produce and the notes are often attractively illustrated. Sadly, the information is probably no better fixed in the memory as the material has not been condensed or key points emphasised.
- The *over-confident student* will look over the notes either in their book or on a revision website online. They will not write

down anything but feel that they 'know it all'. It comes as a nasty shock on exam day when their lack of detailed knowledge lets them down.

The ideal is to focus on the main points and get them firmly into the long-term memory. Students with short-term memory problems cannot expect much help from a quick read through. The best way to reinforce the facts is to use the student's preferred learning style. A range of ideas are listed in Table 13.1 but each student will need to find what works best for them.

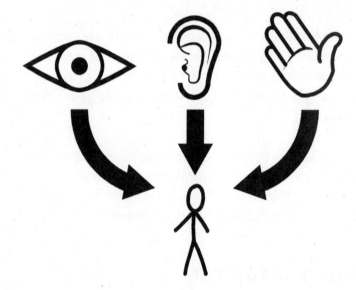

For most people a combination of methods works best. It relieves boredom and keeps the brain actively engaged.

Table 13.1 Learning preferences and revision methods

LEARNING PREFERENCE	REVISION METHODS
Visual	Write out bullet point notes; highlight key words; use mnemonics; make posters of phrases, key words or formulae. Use wipeable white boards.
	Mind maps; cartoons; drawings; flow charts; timelines; use coloured pen or coloured card; make posters illustrating facts or associated ideas.
	Computer programs, revision sites and quizzes are fun, easily accessible and rewarding as they give instant feedback, but care must be taken that they are relevant to a particular exam board and at the correct level.
Auditory	Listen to tapes of set books; read information aloud; self-record and play back; revise with a friend asking and answering questions; convert facts into song, raps, rhythms, poems.
Kinaesthetic (practical)	Use practical examples; let everyday items represent the topic material in order to understand concepts, make 3D models; walk about while reciting; lie on the floor; stand on one leg. Use interactive computer programs.

Revision should be carried out in short blocks of time with breaks for exercise, a snack or a reward. Students' concentration spans vary a great deal, but it is better to do several short sessions of 15 minutes than to sit for two hours staring out of the window and thinking of other things. Mobile phones should be switched off or, preferably, left elsewhere during revision sessions. They are a huge distraction.

It helps to have a few high spots in the programme for each day: 'If I finish my history I can play football.'

Going through past papers with mark schemes is also very useful as it teaches students what is considered important and indicates the depth of knowledge required. The mark allocation normally reflects the number of points needed.

PITFALL 4: GETTING EXHAUSTED

Over-working can be almost as bad as under-working. Students can get tired and stressed and feel overwhelmed by the amount of work. This would especially affect perfectionist students who will be trying to learn everything. Stress can lead to sleep problems, which in turn affect performance and the ability to think clearly and rationally.

Pacing revision and factoring in breaks is important, as is deciding what is essential to learn and which things can be left out.

Last-minute cramming is a bad idea and it is far better to ease off the night before an exam. Students should be encouraged to relax and have an early night.

PITFALL 5: ORGANISATION ON THE EXAM DAY

I have known students who have missed exams owing to misreading the exam timetable. Make sure that they check the date in advance and know whether it is a morning or an afternoon session.

Arriving late can also happen with disorganised students and then they start the exam in a panic. Advise them to allow plenty of time in case there are traffic problems or unforeseen difficulties. Make sure that they know where the exam is being held. This is especially important if they have special arrangements and are not in the main exam room but in another location. They may need to rehearse the route to their exam room.

Remind them to bring the correct equipment. It is always useful to have a spare pencil case, calculator, coloured overlay and whatever else might be needed, in the exam room or school office. It can be lent to a student who forgets something. After all, the exam is based on subject knowledge and not on organisational skills ability.

PITFALL 6: IN THE EXAM

Here are some ideas for students taking exams that are often helpful:

- At the beginning, students should try to relax, wriggle their shoulders and toes, and practise deep breathing.
- They should read the instructions carefully and underline or highlight key words, answering the *right number of questions from the correct sections*. It is very easy to *misread questions*, either altering words or missing out key words altogether, especially with a combination of nervousness and dyslexia.
- Advise students to use a *highlighter or to underline key* words and to read the question twice. Multiple-choice questions can be especially difficult and almost seem to be designed to try to trip the student up.

> I once wrote an excellent answer defining convection complete with diagrams. Sadly, I scored 0 marks. Actually the question was 'What is convention?'
>
> *Author*

- Special notice should be taken of leader words in questions and care should be taken to ensure that an answer reflects these (e.g. describe, evaluate, explain, illustrate, state, summarise). It is an idea to go through these terms with students in advance and explain what each one requires.
- Teach students always to plan long answers and essays. Jotting down ideas and making rough plans are invaluable strategies, especially for students with short-term memory problems or 'grasshopper minds'. It is also worth re-reading the question again before starting to write to make sure that the answer is relevant.

- Timing in the exam – mistiming is a common fault, especially in essay subjects. Some students are slow to write or to process information. Others lose concentration and time passes while they are thinking of other things. Some may give too much detail in one question and then have to rush the others. Time prompts can now be given at intervals in public exams.

- Perfectionist students will be loath to move on until an answer is excellent. They may even cross the whole thing out and start again. Some students may benefit from periodic time prompts to remind them of their remaining exam time.

- All students should be able to see a digital clock clearly as they are no longer allowed to wear watches in public exams (this is because many watches have other electronic functions such as memory, calculator, thesaurus etc.)

- Check work at the end. Students should look out for number reversals in maths answers and check that units are correct.

- Extra time – if this is has been allowed, the students must be taught how to use it properly, especially for thinking and planning. They should also have practised with extra time in school tests and exams.

PITFALL 7: AFTER THE EXAM

Students should avoid conducting a 'post mortem' of the paper with others. It is too late to do anything about any mistakes and it can cause anguish and undermine self-confidence. It is important to keep morale up and stay cheerful, especially if another exam is imminent.

Avoid dwelling on any mistakes. It is better to move on to the next thing. Most students who lack self-confidence ignore the large number of things that they may have done correctly and worry about any errors.

Encourage the students to relax for a while, to eat and get some fresh air and exercise. This will 'recharge the batteries' and allow clear thinking before the next exam or revision session.

SPECIAL ARRANGEMENTS IN PUBLIC EXAMS

Many students with SpLDs or medical diagnoses will qualify for special arrangements in public exams.

The rules and special arrangements are complex and change periodically so the school SENCO (special educational needs coordinator) will work with the exams officer to ensure that the provision that has been recommended is carried out. In the UK, regulations are printed by the Joint Council for Qualifications (JCQ). These are regularly updated.

The list of possible special arrangements is long but here are some of the most common ones found in mainstream schools:

- Extra time (usually 25 per cent, but it can be longer in special circumstances) – can be for slow writing or processing speed.
- Supervised rest breaks.
- Separate invigilation away from the other students (a candidate who is in a separate room may also be allowed to read out loud or walk around the room).
- Coloured or enlarged papers.
- A word processor with the spelling and grammar checker disabled.
- A scribe (amanuensis) – a responsible adult who will write down the candidate's dictated answers.
- An electronic voice-to-text programme set on exam mode.
- A reader – a responsible adult who reads the question paper out to the candidate (they are not permitted to explain or interpret any of the paper).
- An electronic text-to-voice programme set on exam mode.
- A reader pen adapted for exam use.
- A practical assistant – a responsible adult who can give physical support for students with severe coordination difficulties.
- A prompter – a responsible adult who periodically reminds the candidate how much exam time is left.

In all the cases listed the student must show a history of using these techniques in their normal lessons and in school exams. This gives them a chance to practise the skills and will provide both a history of need and a history of provision which is required by the JCQ. Classroom teachers should be aware of the provision that is recommended for a student to ensure that the advice is followed as normal classroom practice.

KEY POINTS

- Exams are especially stressful times for students with learning differences.
- Planning a revision schedule is important.
- Students must learn revision techniques using their preferred learning style and pace themselves sensibly.
- Students must check when and where the exams take place.
- Bringing the correct equipment is important, but it is useful to have spares for emergencies in school.
- During exams students must concentrate on reading instructions and questions carefully and take notice of the leader words in questions.
- Timing and planning are important, especially if a student has extra time.
- After exams it is important to relax and not to over-analyse any perceived errors.
- Special arrangements can be put in place in public exams.

CHAPTER 14

A Final Word

Thankfully, many neurodivergent young people are now diagnosed early and receive the additional help that they need to negotiate their way successfully through their schooldays. Sadly, some are still not spotted, and it is often an astute teacher who identifies them. Watch out for discrepancies in a student's intelligence and performance and, if you are concerned, ask the SENCO to investigate further. Girls are especially likely to be missed as they may try to mask their symptoms in order to blend in with the crowd and pass unnoticed.

There are many stories of unusual thinkers who have gone on to lead happy and successful lives. With the correct support at school and university many are now following conventional careers, such as medicine, engineering and teaching. Others have diversified and have become inspirational leaders in their fields. If you consider the current entrepreneurs, graphic designers, computer programmers, actors, film directors, authors, sporting legends, chefs or leaders in fashion, many will be people who have an unusual way of thinking and for whom learning at school was a struggle. Today, some employers are actively trying to introduce neurodiversity into their teams. Autistic people often have a great eye for detail, while holistic thinkers have unusual ideas and approaches to problem solving. Both have an important role to play.

The advantage of thinking differently enables people to see new opportunities and unusual paths to follow. Ultimately it is their thinking differences that help to shape their lives and make them who they are. Their success may well be not 'in spite of' their learning differences but 'because of' them.

If you, as a teacher, can help and support these young people enabling them to be proud of their strengths and learn how to laugh when things go wrong, you will have contributed hugely to launching the adults that they will become. Their thinking differences will never go away, but they can learn coping strategies and fortitude, enabling them to channel their many skills and talents and to maximise their potential.

As teachers, we should encourage these young people who think a little differently, and enjoy their company. I can guarantee that they will be annoying, challenging and frustrating at times, but they may well be the students you will remember most fondly.

Glossary

Amanuensis: A person who writes from dictation.

Asperger syndrome: Previous term for an ASD Level 1 diagnosis.

Assistive technology: Device, piece of equipment or system that helps bypass, work around or compensate for an individual's specific learning difficulties.

Attention deficit hyperactivity disorder (ADHD): A disorder which causes a short attention span, impulsiveness and sometimes increased physical activity (hyperactivity). It is a result of reduced activity in the frontal lobe area of the brain.

Auditory learning: Learning by taking in information that has been heard.

Auditory memory: The ability to remember information that has been heard.

Auditory processing speed: The time to take in information that has been heard, to think about it and be able to respond.

Autism spectrum disorder (ASD): People with a diagnosis of ASD have communication and social difficulties and restricted, repetitive patterns of behaviour and interests.

CAMHS (Child and Adolescent Mental Health Services): Medical services that support and treat young people experiencing mental health problems. They work with schools, charities and local authorities. They can diagnose medical conditions such as ADHD or ASD.

Cognitive behavioural therapy (CBT): Treatment that aims to solve problems by talking about them with a therapist and gradually changing how people think and behave. It can be useful to treat anxiety and depression, OCD and ADHD.

Compulsion: Ritual behaviour which a person with OCD feels that they have to carry out in order to prevent bad things from happening to themselves or to others.

Computer reader in an exam: Computer software which accurately reads out text, but does not decode or interpret the paper.

Coprolalia: Involuntary outburst of swearing, obscene words or socially inappropriate remarks. Affects approximately 10 per cent of people with Tourettes.

Developmental coordination disorder (DCD, also called dyspraxia): A Specific Learning Difference involving muscles and fine or gross motor coordination. Symptoms include difficulty with movement as well as problems with organisation, short-term memory and planning.

Dyscalculia: A Specific Learning Difference that affects mathematical skills, especially arithmetic and counting.

Dysgraphia: A Specific Learning Difference that affects handwriting and converting thoughts to written words.

Dyslexia: A Specific Learning Difference that affects reading and interpretation of the written word together with spelling and converting ideas into writing.

Dyspraxia: See developmental coordination disorder (DCD).

Echolalia: When another person's spoken word is repeated, or repeating the same word over and over.

Education, Health and Care Plan (EHCP): Legal document outlining support for a child that the local authority must provide in addition to support provided by the school.

Empathy: An understanding of how other people feel.

Executive function: Higher levels of brain function, such as paying attention, using the working memory, decision making, planning and setting goals and targets.

Frontal lobes: The front part of the brain responsible for reasoned logical behaviour, initiative, planning and personality.

Glue ear: A condition that can occur in children. The middle ear becomes filled with a sticky fluid as a result of infection; this may result in partial hearing loss. Implicated in dyslexia as sounds (phonemes) are not heard accurately in childhood.

Holistic learner: Likes to see the whole picture before concentrating on the detail.

Individual Education Plan (IEP): School-based plan to support a pupil who has special needs.

Interpersonal skills: The ability to relate to others and to work well in group situations.

Intrapersonal skills: The ability to work effectively alone and be self-reliant.

Kinaesthetic learning: Taking in and remembering information by doing – involves moving, handling materials, carrying out experiments.

Long-term memory: Information that is stored for months or years and can be recalled when needed.

Masking: When a person tries to cover up any behavioural differences in order to fit in socially.

Meltdown: A physical response due to increasing anxiety in an overwhelming situation. Can include shouting, hysteria and aggression.

Mnemonic: A learning technique using phrases to help remember a spelling or an order of events or things.

Neurodivergent: People who have brain functions, ways of processing information (thinking style) and behaviours that are outside the normal or standard range.

Neurodiversity: Variations in brain functions, ways of processing information (thinking style) and behaviours within the population as a whole.

Neurotransmitters: Special chemicals that transfer impulses from one nerve cell (neuron) to another across tiny gaps called synapses.

Obsessions: Unwanted intrusive thoughts and fears.

Obsessive compulsive disorder (OCD): Experience of recurrent disturbing fears that are irrational and intrusive. Compulsions are an attempt to relieve anxiety by repeating certain actions.

Oppositional defiant disorder (ODD): Psychological disorder affecting behaviour. Children with ODD are uncooperative, defiant, and hostile towards peers, parents, teachers and other authority figures.

Pathological demand avoidance (PDA): Anxiety-induced trait shown by some autistic students. Will try to avoid perceived demands.

Personal, social and health education (PSHE): This is taught in most schools. Emphasises understanding, tolerance and embracing differences.

Phoneme: A small set of speech sounds that are distinguished by the speakers of a particular language. They can be single letters or blends of consonants or vowels such as 'ch', 'th' or 'oa'.

Processing speed: The time taken to absorb information and to think about a response.

Reading pen: Hand-held device that will scan and read out words or sentences.

Scaffolding: Providing temporary support for a learner in order to help them to complete a task or acquire a skill, and then gradually withdrawing that support.

Short-term memory (working memory): The ability to remember information for a short while in order to use it. For example, remembering numbers in a maths calculation. The information is then forgotten.

Special educational needs (SEN): Refers to children with learning problems that make it harder for them to learn than most children the same age.

Special educational needs and disability (SEND): Refers to children with physical disabilities as well as those with learning problems.

Special educational needs coordinator (SENCO): A teacher who has responsibility for the day-to-day management of special educational needs in a school.

Specific Learning Difficulty (SpLD): A range of problems that some people have in one area of learning while they can perform well or even excel in other areas. It does not affect the overall intelligence of the person.

Stimming: (self-stimulatory behaviour): Repetitive movements, words or noises carried out by some autistic people when they try to control a build-up of emotion.

Subitising: The ability to recognise small number patterns without counting (e.g. dots on a dice).

Theory of mind: The ability to see things from someone else's point of view, to understand their behaviour and predict their reactions.

Tics: Sudden involuntary twitches, movements or sounds that people do repeatedly.

Tourette syndrome: A condition that causes people to make involuntary movements or sounds called tics.

Tracking: The ability to coordinate the action of the two eyes to follow a line of print.

Trigger: Something that initiates anxiety and an obsessional thought.

Visual memory: The ability to remember and recall information that has been seen.

Visual processing: The time it takes to respond to information which has been seen.

Visual stress: A visual problem where the eyes do not work correctly together; can cause print distortion, reading difficulties and headaches. Distance vision can be normal so it is sometimes missed.

Working memory: See short-term memory.

Summary table of most common areas of difficulty

	DYSLEXIA	DYSCALCULIA	DYSGRAPHIA	DYSPRAXIA/DCD	ASD/ASPERGER	ADHD	OCD	TOURETTES
Spelling	■							
Reading	■							
Reading comprehension	■				■			
Number confusion	■	■		■				
Letter confusion	■		■					
Symbol confusion	■	■						
Short-term memory	■					■		
Can be distracted	■					■	■	■
Poor organisation	■			■		■		
Gets lost	■			■		■		
Time keeping	■			■		■		
Likes order/detail					■		■	
Need to move around				■	■	■		■
Fine coordination			■	■				■
Gross coordination				■				■
Social skills				■	■	■		
Literal translation				■	■			
Routines/rituals				■	■		■	
Special interests				■	■			
Obsessions							■	
Compulsions							■	■

Remember, many students will not show all the characteristics listed. Also, some students will have more than one condition.

Comparison of PDA and ODD

PDA Pathological Demand Avoidance	ODD *Oppositional Defiant Disorder*
Part of the autism spectrum	*Not part of the autism spectrum*
Driven by anxiety and not deliberately antagonistic	*Psychological drive to be antagonistic*
Tries to talk their way out of demands initially	*Persistent defiance and irritability*
Creative avoidance techniques	*Simply refuses or does the opposite*
Social communication differences	*Competent social understanding*
Can be aggressive if highly stressed or carry out self-harm	*Possible aggression and spitefulness*
Resists all demands	*Resists only specific things*
Incentive-based rewards not effective	*Incentive-based rewards effective*
Driven to avoid demands due to high anxiety about not feeling in control	*Driven by persistent negative and hostile attitudes towards authority*
Traditional parenting/teaching/support ineffective	*Traditional strategies often work*
Emotional meltdowns when stressed by demands	*Temper tantrums and conflicts*
Sociable	*Rude, criticises others*
Avoidance behaviour variable due to differing stress levels	*Antagonistic behaviour in general, but can be modified with incentives*
Responds to more open teaching style giving more options	*Responds to fewer commands and more collaboration*

Downloadable quick teacher checklists of indicators of the most common learning differences

☑ QUICK TEACHER CHECK: INDICATORS OF DYSLEXIA

Overall

- ☐ A discrepancy between oral contribution and understanding with written work
- ☐ Underperforms in timed tests and exams
- ☐ Slow processing speed with written material
- ☐ Does not finish timed exams
- ☐ Imaginative, creative

Reading

- ☐ Inaccurate, misreads words, substitutes for similar words
- ☐ Misses out words or lines or repeats them
- ☐ Difficulty comprehending meaning of a passage, may have to read it several times
- ☐ Letter or number reversal when reading
- ☐ Difficulty following instructions
- ☐ Hesitant, laboured especially when reading aloud

Spelling

- ☐ Inaccurate
- ☐ May spell the same word differently in the same passage
- ☐ Can do well at spelling tests but comes 'unstuck' when concentrating on writing
- ☐ Misses out middle of words
- ☐ Spells phonetically

Writing

- ☐ Poor quality compared with oral ability
- ☐ Can be imaginative and thoughtful but spelling and comprehension poor and variable
- ☐ Capital letters used randomly
- ☐ Some letters reversed (e.g. *d* and *b*)

Organisation

- ☐ Easily distracted
- ☐ Forgetful
- ☐ Loses belongings
- ☐ Confuses left and right
- ☐ Gets lost easily
- ☐ Problems reading the time, timetables and instructions
- ☐ Difficulty organising ideas clearly and logically

N.B. This sheet is not intended to give a diagnosis but if a significant number of these indicators are shown it could be worth suggesting further diagnostic investigation.

☑ QUICK TEACHER CHECK: INDICATORS OF DYSCALCULIA

Overall

- ☐ Articulate and good verbally and but struggles with tasks involving numbers and calculations
- ☐ Written work much better than numerical work
- ☐ Problems remembering sequences of numbers such as phone numbers
- ☐ Liable to guess numerical answers
- ☐ Lacks confidence in numerical ability

Numbers

- ☐ Misreads or reverses numbers (e.g. 35 becomes 53)
- ☐ Problems relating numbers in size order – which is larger?
- ☐ Cannot easily estimate numbers, has to count
- ☐ Difficulty rounding up or down
- ☐ Problems with zeros and decimal points
- ☐ Difficulty counting backwards
- ☐ Finds it hard to count in sets of numbers e.g. x2, x5, x10
- ☐ Problems learning tables
- ☐ Difficulty seeing connections (e.g. 7 x 3 = 21 then 3 x 7 = 21)
- ☐ Difficulty with fractions and decimal points

Mathematical procedures

- ☐ Unsure if a procedure will make the answer bigger or smaller
- ☐ Slow at mental arithmetic
- ☐ Slow to work out calculations
- ☐ May count on fingers
- ☐ If procedures are learned they are followed mechanically without understanding or confidence
- ☐ Problems remembering formulae
- ☐ Scales on graphs inaccurate
- ☐ Difficulty using equations

Life skills, problems with the following

- ☐ Money: calculating change and counting quickly when shopping
- ☐ Telling time and getting to places punctually
- ☐ Reading timetables

N.B. This sheet is not intended to give a diagnosis but if a significant number of these indicators are shown it could be worth suggesting further diagnostic investigation.

☑ QUICK TEACHER CHECK: INDICATORS OF DYSPRAXIA

Overall

- ☐ Appearance slightly untidy/scruffy: shirt hanging out, shoelaces undone, buttons incorrectly done up, clothes may be stained from spills
- ☐ Good IT skills producing work markedly better than written work
- ☐ Unconventional lateral thinker

Gross coordination

- ☐ Clumsiness: liable to drop things, spill, trip, fall off chair
- ☐ Poor spatial awareness: bumps into objects, furniture or other people
- ☐ Difficulty with ball games
- ☐ Fidgets in class
- ☐ Balance problems

Fine coordination

- ☐ Poor handwriting and drawing skills: crossing out, ink blotches, writing not on lines.
- ☐ Work produced of a much lower than expected standard compared to oral contribution in class or work produced on a computer
- ☐ Struggles to use instruments (e.g. scissors, burettes, pouring water)
- ☐ Slow to dress: problems with buttons, ties, shoelaces

Memory and organisation

- ☐ Poor short-term memory: forgets instructions
- ☐ Forgets to bring correct books or equipment to lessons, fails to hand in homework
- ☐ Arrives late
- ☐ Goes to wrong place or right place at wrong time
- ☐ Books and files out of order
- ☐ Difficulty with time management

Sense perception

- ☐ Over- or under-sensitive to certain smells, textures, temperature, sounds or lights

Social/personal

- ☐ Difficulty reading social situations
- ☐ May stand too near others or too far away
- ☐ Difficulty reading body language
- ☐ Poor personal hygiene

N.B. This sheet is not intended to give a diagnosis but if a significant number of these indicators are shown it could be worth suggesting further diagnostic investigation.

☑ QUICK TEACHER CHECK: INDICATORS OF ADHD

Overall

☐ Short concentration span
☐ Full of ideas and enthusiasm
☐ Difficulty completing tasks
☐ Underachieves
☐ Poor short-term memory

Inattentive symptoms

☐ Makes careless mistakes due to lack of close attention to detail
☐ Easily distracted by extraneous stimuli
☐ May not appear to listen when spoken to directly
☐ Has difficulty sustaining attention in tasks or activities
☐ Fails to complete tasks or follow instructions fully
☐ Is reluctant to engage in schoolwork or homework requiring sustained mental effort.
☐ Prefers quick tasks with instant feedback (e.g. computer quizzes)
☐ Difficulty in organisation and prioritising tasks
☐ Loses equipment, books, notes, pens
☐ Fails to hand in homework

Hyperactive – impulsive symptoms

☐ Enthusiastic and always ready to volunteer
☐ Talks excessively
☐ Does not listen to others
☐ Interrupts the teacher or other students
☐ Has difficulty waiting to take their turn
☐ Blurts out answers
☐ Fidgets with hands or equipment
☐ Does not sit still
☐ Leaves the seat in situations when remaining in seat is expected
☐ Runs about or climbs inappropriately
☐ Has difficulty working in groups

Based on the symptoms, three subtypes of ADHD can occur:

☐ Primarily inattentive – more prevalent in girls
☐ Primarily hyperactive impulsive
☐ Combined subtype

N.B. This sheet is not intended to give a diagnosis but if a significant number of these indicators are shown it could be worth suggesting further diagnostic investigation.

☑ QUICK TEACHER CHECK: INDICATORS OF ASD

Overall

☐ Socially awkward
☐ Finds friendship and social encounters difficult
☐ Direct way of talking
☐ Very knowledgeable on some topics

Speech

☐ Literal interpretation
☐ Pedantic
☐ Does not pick up unspoken signals
☐ Large vocabulary especially on certain topics
☐ May dominate conversation
☐ Likes to use long words
☐ Does not pick up implied or inferred meanings

Special interest

☐ Very knowledgeable about particular interest
☐ May have collections of items

Sensory

☐ Either over- or under-sensitive to particular textures, sounds, lights, smells, taste

Social

☐ Dislikes crowds, close contact
☐ Difficulty reading social situations, finds them stressful
☐ Difficulty seeing other people's point of view
☐ Struggles to work well in groups
☐ Likes routines
☐ Finds social conversation difficult
☐ Will often not understand puns or jokes

Temper

☐ Anxiety and sensory overload can lead to temper outbursts

N.B. This sheet is not intended to give a diagnosis but if a significant number of these indicators are shown it could be worth suggesting further diagnostic investigation.

☑ QUICK TEACHER CHECK: INDICATORS OF OCD

The obsessions and compulsions vary widely and so it is difficult to make a definitive list of indicators, but these are some common traits. It is also worth remembering that OCD is often concurrent with other conditions.

Overall

☐ Anxious

☐ Repetitive behaviours

☐ Frequent, prolonged toilet visits due to completing rituals

☐ Inability to touch certain items

☐ Arranging items so they are aligned

☐ Tiredness, lateness due to performing rituals

☐ Crossing out and re-writing work

☐ Excessive questioning for reassurance

Common obsessions

☐ Fears about dirt and contamination

☐ Worries about harm coming to others or themselves

☐ Thoughts about doing something forbidden

☐ Discomfort if things are not even and symmetrical

☐ Fears of losing important items

☐ Needs to tell, ask or confess

Common compulsions

☐ Checking and re-checking things

☐ Touching or tapping certain things in a special way

☐ Washing and cleaning

☐ Arranging things so they are 'just right'

☐ Collecting things that are useless

☐ Seeking reassurance

☐ Counting, repeating and re-doing things

N.B. This sheet is not intended to give a diagnosis but if a significant number of these indicators are shown it could be worth suggesting further diagnostic investigation.

References, websites and support organisations

CHAPTER 1: BRAINS THAT WORK A LITTLE DIFFERENTLY

References

Worthington, A. (ed.) (2003) *The Fulton Special Education Digest*. London: David Fulton Publishers.

Further reading

Gathercole, S. and Packiam Alloway, T. (2008) *Working Memory and Learning: A Practical Guide for Teachers*. London: Sage Publications.

Honeybourne, V. (2018) *The Neurodiverse Classroom*. London: Jessica Kingsley Publishers.

Kerchner, G.A. (2014) 'What causes the brain to have slow processing speed?' *Scientific American Mind 25*, 2, March.

Patrick, A. (2020) *The Memory and Processing Guide for Neurodiverse Learners*. London: Jessica Kingsley Publishers.

Specialist software

British Dyslexia Association technology advice: https://bdanewtechnologies.wordpress.com

Dyslexia Tool Kit: www.educationalappstore.com/app/dyslexia-tool-kit

Texthelp: www.texthelp.com/en-gb

- ClaroRead: www.texthelp.com/en-gb/solutions/dsa/claroread
- Read&Write: www.texthelp.com/products/read-and-write-education
- Global AutoCorrect: www.texthelp.com/en-gb/solutions/dsa/global-autocorrect

CHAPTER 2: DYSLEXIA

References

British Dyslexia Association (n.d.) 'Dyslexia.' www.bdadyslexia.org.uk/dyslexia

Rose, J. (2009) *Identifying and Teaching Children and Young People with Dyslexia and Literacy Difficulties*. Report to the Secretary of State. London: Department for Children, Schools and Families

Schnep, M.H.H. (2014) 'The advantages of dyslexia: With reading difficulties can come other cognitive strengths.' *Scientific American*. 19 August. www.scientificamerican.com/article/the-advantages-of-dyslexia

Further reading

Bennett, J. (2013) *Dyslexia Pocketbook* (2nd edn). Alresford: Teachers' Pocketbooks.

Eide, B.L. and Eide, F. (2023) *The Dyslexic Advantage*. Carlsbad, CA: Hay House.

Goodwin, J. (2012) *Studying with Dyslexia*. London: Palgrave Macmillan.

Griggs, K. (2021) *This Is Dyslexia*. London: Vermilion.

Hodge P. (2000) 'A Dyslexic Child in the classroom: A guide for teachers and parents.' www.dyslexia.com/library/classroom.htm

Hudson, D. (2019) 'Travelling with Dyslexia – why people with dyslexia get lost.' *SEN Magazine*, 25 July. https://senmagazine.co.uk/content/specific-needs/dyslexia-spld/7791/travelling-with-dyslexia

Hudson, D. (2021) *Exploring Science with Dyslexic Children and Teens*. London: Jessica Kingsley Publishers.

Hultquist, A. (2013) *Can I Tell You About Dyslexia?* London: Jessica Kingsley Publishers.

Pavey B., Meehan, M. and Davis, S. (2013) *The Dyslexia-Friendly Teacher's Toolkit*. London: Sage Publications.

Reid, G. (2019) *Dyslexia and Inclusion: Classroom Approaches for Assessment, Teaching and Learning*. London: David Fulton Publishers.

Reid, G. and Green, S. (2011) *100 Ideas for Supporting Pupils with Dyslexia*. London: Continuum.

Resources and information

Barrington Stoke, publisher producing books specifically designed for readers with dyslexia: www.barringtonstoke.co.uk

Crossbow Education: www.crossboweducation.com

Fun-with-words: www.fun-with-words.com

Made by Dyslexia: www.madebydyslexia.org

Wordshark, spelling and reading program: www.wordshark.co.uk

Assistive technology software

Iansyst: www.iansyst.co.uk/technology

Inclusive Technology: www.inclusive.co.uk/software/dyslexia-software

Support organisations

British Dyslexia Association: www.bdadyslexia.org.uk

Dyslexia Action: www.dyslexiaaction.org.uk

Helen Arkell Dyslexia Centre, a specialist teaching centre: https://helenarkell.org.uk/

CHAPTER 3: DYSCALCULIA

References

British Dyslexia Association (n.d.) 'Dyscalculia.' www.bdadyslexia.org.uk/dyscalculia

Further reading

Babtie, P. and Dillion, S, (2019) *100 ideas for Secondary Teachers Supporting Students with Numeracy Difficulties*. London. Bloomsbury.

Bird, R. (2013) *The Dyscalculia Toolkit: Supporting Learning Difficulties in Maths*. London: Paul Chapman Publishers.

Butterworth, B. (2018) *Dyscalculia: From Science to Education*. London: Routledge.

Butterworth, B. (2022) *Can Fish Count?* London: Quercus Books.

Chinn, S. (2018) *Maths Learning Difficulties and Dyscalculia* (2nd edn). London: BDA.

Chinn, S. and Ashcroft J.R. (2017) *Mathematics for Dyslexics Including Dyscalculia: A Teaching Handbook* (4th edn). London: Wiley.

Emerson, J. and Babtie, P. (2014) *The Dyscalculia Solution: Teaching Number Sense*. London: Bloomsbury.

Hannell, G. (2015) *Dyscalculia: Action Plans for Successful Learning in Mathematics*. London: David Fulton Publishers.

Hornigold, J.(2015) *Dyscalculia Pocketbook*. Alresford: Teachers' Pocketbooks.

Hornigold, J. (2017) *Understanding Maths Learning Difficulties* Oxford: Oxford University Press.

Moorcraft, P. (2014) *It Just Doesn't Add Up*. Croydon: Filament Publishing.

Resources and information

Brain Balance, ways to help children with dyscalculia: www.brainbalancecenters.com/blog/practical-ways-parents-can-help-child-dyscalculia

Cambridge House, maths resources and 3D shapes: https://issuu.com/cambridgesen/docs/cambridge_house_2019_catalogue

Crossbow Education, teaching-resources: www.crossboweducation.com/maths-and-dyscalculia-teaching-resources

Equatio (produced by Texthelp), the maths versions of Read&Write: www.texthelp.com/en-gb/products/equatio

IDL numeracy software: https://idlsgroup.com/numeracy

Maths games: www.freeteacher.co.uk

Maths games: www.topmarks.co.uk/maths-games/11-14-years/number

Numbershark, computer maths games: www.wordshark.co.uk/numbershark

Numicon, maths resources: www.numicon.co.nz

TES dyscalculia awareness poster: www.tes.com/teaching-resource/dyscalculia-awareness-poster-6340458

TTS dyscalculia resources for schools: www.tts-group.co.uk/secondary/sen/dyscalculia

Support organisations

British Dyslexia Association: www.bdadyslexia.org.uk/dyscalculia

Dyscalculia Association: www.dyscalculiaassociation.uk

National Numeracy: www.nationalnumeracy.org.uk/what-numeracy/what-dyscalculia

The Dyscalculia information Centre: www.dyscalculia.me.uk/teachers.html

The Dyscalculia Network: www.dyscalculianetwork.com

CHAPTER 4: DYSGRAPHIA

References

American Psychiatric Association (2013) *Diagnostic and Statistical Manual of Mental Disorders* (5th edn). Arlington, VA: American Psychiatric Publishing.

Cleveland Clinic (2022) 'Dysgraphia.' https://my.clevelandclinic.org/health/diseases/23294-dysgraphia

Further reading

Bennett, J. (2007) *Handwriting Pocketbook*. Alresford: Teachers' Pocketbooks.

Bryce, B. and Stephens, B. (2014) *The Dysgraphia Sourcebook: Everything You Need to Help Your Child*. CreateSpace Independent Publishing Platform.

Child, B. (2021) *Dysgraphia Papers for Kids: A Handwriting Workbook*. BrainChild

Dotterer, C. (2018) *Handwriting Brain-Body DisConnect*. Author Academy Elite.

Sutherland, J. and Green, M. (eds) (2014) Dysgraphia: Causes, Connections and Cures. CreateSpace Independent Publishing Platform.

Resources and information

Back in Action, desk height adjusters, writing slopes, posture packs: www.backinaction.co.uk/computers

Crossbow Education, writing aids, pen grips: www.crossboweducation.Com/shop-now/handwriting-resources

DyslexiaA2Z: https://dyslexiaa2z.com/learning-difficulties/dysgraphia

Stabilo easy pens, shaped pens for easy writing: www.stabilo.com/uk

The Good Schools Guide to Dysgraphia: www.goodschoolsguide.co.uk/special-educational-needs/types-of-sen/dysgraphia

Yoropen, ergonomic pens: www.yoropen.com/en/index.html

Support organisations

Dyslexia SPELD Foundation: https://dsf.net.au/what-is-dysgraphia

Understood organisation: www.understood.org/en/articles/understanding-dysgraphia

CHAPTER 5: DYSPRAXIA/DCD

References

Dyspraxia Foundation (2015) 'Dyspraxia – "Is it a battle of the sexes?"' https://dyspraxiafoundation.org.uk/news-archive/dyspraxia-is-battle-sexes

Movement Matters (2012) 'What is developmental coordination disorder/dyspraxia?' https://movementmattersuk.org/what-is-developmental-coordination-disorder-dyspraxia

Further reading

Biggs, V. (2014) *Caged in Chaos: A Dyspraxic Guide to Breaking Free.* London: Jessica Kingsley Publishers.

Boon, M. (2014) *Can I Tell You About My Dyspraxia?* London: Jessica Kingsley Publishers.

Christmas, J. and van de Weyer, R. (2019) *Hands on Dyspraxia: Developmental Coordination Disorder: Supporting Young People with Motor and Sensory Challenges.* London: Routledge.

Hoopman, K. (2022) *All About Dyspraxia.* London: Jessica Kingsley Publishers.

Kirby, A. (2009) *Dyspraxia: Developmental and Cooordination Disorder (DCD)* (8th edn). London: Souvenir Press.

Kirby, A. and Peters, L. (2007) *100 Ideas for Supporting Pupils with Dyspraxia and DCD.* London: Continuum.

Lloyd, S. and Graham, L. (2022) *Developmental Coordination Disorder (Dyspraxia): How to Help.* London: Pavilion Publishing.

Patrick, A. (2015) *The Dyspraxic Learner: Strategies for Success.* London: Jessica Kingsley Publishers.

Talukdar, A. (2012) *Dyspraxia/DCD Pocketbook.* Alresford: Teachers' Pocketbooks.

Resources and information

Back in Action, desk height adjusters, writing slopes, posture packs: www.backinaction.co.uk/computers

Movement Matters: www.movementmattersuk.org

Patient (health information website): https://patient.info/childrens-health/dyspraxia-developmental-co-ordination-disorder

Stabilo easy pens, shaped pens for easy writing: www.stabilo.com/uk

Yoropen ergonomic pens: www.yoropen.com/en/index.html

Support organisations

Dyspraxia Association of Ireland: www.dyspraxia.ie

Dyspraxia Foundation: https://dyspraxiafoundation.org.uk

CHAPTER 6: ATTENTION DEFICIT HYPERACTIVITY DISORDER

References

American Psychiatric Association (2013) *Diagnostic and Statistical Manual of Mental Disorders* (5th edn). Arlington, VA: American Psychiatric Publishing.

NHS Choices (n.d.) 'Attention deficit hyperactivity disorder (ADHD).' www.nhs.uk/conditions/Attention-deficit-hyperactivity-disorder

Further reading

Ali, S. (2022) *The Teenage Girls Guide to Living Well with ADHD*. London. Jessica Kingsley Publishers.

Hallowell, M. and Ratey, M. (2022) *ADHD 2.0*. New York, NY: Ballantine Books.

Kewley, G. and Latham, P. (2008) *100 Ideas for Supporting Pupils with ADHD*. London: Continuum.

Nunn, T., Hanstock, T. and Lask, B. (2008) *Who's Who of the Brain*. London: Jessica Kingsley Publishers.

O'Regan, F. (2019) *Successfully Teaching and Managing Children with ADHD: A Resource for SENCOs and Teachers*. London Routledge.

Swietzer, L. (2014) *The Elephant in the ADHD Room*. London: Jessica Kingsley Publishers.

Thompson, A. (2016) *The Boy from Hell: Life with a Child with ADHD*. Farringdon: Proof Fairy Publishers.

Support organisations

ADDISS, the National Attention Deficit Disorder Information and Support Service: www.addiss.co.uk

ADHD Foundation: www.adhdfoundation.org.uk

ADHD Kids, support organisation for parents and children: http://adhdkids.org.uk

ADHD UK: https://adhduk.co.uk

UK ADHD Partnership: www.ukadhd.com/index.htm

CHAPTER 7: AUTISM SPECTRUM DISORDER

References

American Psychiatric Association (2013) *Diagnostic and Statistical Manual of Mental Disorders* (5th edn). Arlington, VA: American Psychiatric Publishing.

Jackson, L. (2002) *Freaks, Geeks and Asperger Syndrome*. London: Jessica Kingsley Publishers.

Further reading

Ansell, G. (2011) Working with Asperger Syndrome in the Classroom: An Insider's Guide. London: Jessica Kingsley Publishers.

Brady, F. (2023) *Strong Female Character*. London: Octopus Publishing Group Ltd.

Brower, F. (2014) *100 ideas for Supporting Pupils on the Autistic Spectrum*. London: Continuum.

Egerton, J. and Carpenter, B. (2016) *Girls and Autism Flying Under the Radar*. Tamworth: Nasen Publishers.

Hartman, D. (2020) *The Little Book of Autism FAQs: How to Talk to Your Child About Their Diagnosis*. London: Jessica Kingsley Publishers.

Hoopman, K. (2015) *The Essential MI for Asperger Syndrome (ASD) in the Classroom*. London: Jessica Kingsley Publishers.

McCann, L. (2017) *How to Support Students with Autism Spectrum Disorder in Secondary School*. Hyde: LDA.

Notbohm, E. (2019) *Ten Things Every Child with Autism Wishes You Knew*. Arlington, TX: Future Horizons.

Torrence, J. (2018) *Therapeutic Adventures with Autistic Children*. London: Jessica Kingsley Publishers.

Willey, L.H. (2015) *Pretending to be Normal: Living with Asperger Syndrome* (2nd edn). London: Jessica Kingsley Publishers.

Wood, R. with Crane, L. Happé, F. Morrison, A. and Moyse, R. (2022) *Learning from Autistic Teachers*. London. Jessica Kingsley Publishers.

Resources

ASD visual aids: www.asdvisualaids.com

Support organisations

Ambitious about Autism: www.ambitiousaboutautism.org.uk

ASPEN (Autism, Educational Network): www.aspennj.org

Autistic Girls Network: https://autisticgirlsnetwork.org

Child Autism UK: www.childautism.org.uk

National Autistic Society: www.autism.org.uk

CHAPTER 8: PATHOLOGICAL DEMAND AVOIDANCE

References

American Psychiatric Association (2013) *Diagnostic and Statistical Manual of Mental Disorders* (5th edn). Arlington, VA: American Psychiatric Publishing.

World Health Organization (2019) *International Statistical Classification of Diseases and Related Health Problems* (11th revision). www.who.int/standards/classifications/classification-of-diseases

Further reading

Fidler, R. and Christie, P. (2015) *Can I Tell You About My Pathological Demand Avoidance Syndrome?* London: Jessica Kingsley Publishers.

Fidler, R. and Christie, P.(2019) *Collaborative Approaches to Learning for Pupils with PDA*. London: Jessica Kingsley Publishers.

Newson, E., Le Marechal, K. and David, C. (2003) 'Pathological demand avoidance syndrome: A necessary distinction with pervasive development disorders.' *Archives of Diseases in Childhood 88,* 595–600.

Truman, C. (2021) *The Teacher's Introduction to Pathological Demand Avoidance*. London: Jessica Kingsley Publishers.

Support organisations

National Autistic Society: www.autism.org.uk

PDA Society: www.pdasociety.org.uk

CHAPTER 9: SENSORY PROCESSING DISORDER

Further reading

Allen, S. (2016) *Can I Tell You About My Sensory Processing Difficulties?* London: Jessica Kingsley Publishers.

Biel, L. and Pes, N. (2009) *Raising a Sensory Smart Child*. New York, NY: Penguin.

Mill, L. and Fuller, D. (2007) *Sensational Kids: Hope and Help for Children with Sensory Processing*. New York, NY: Penguin.

Whitney, R. and Gibbs, V. (2020) *Raising Kids with Sensory Disorders*. London: Routledge.

Thoonsen, T. and Lamp, C. (2021) *Sensory Solutions in the Classroom: The Teacher's Guide to Fidgeting, Inattention and Restlessness.* London: Jessica Kingsley Publishers.

Resources and information

ADDitude: www.additudemag.com/slideshows/what-is-sensory-processing-disorder

CAMHS North Derbyshire: www.camhsnorthderbyshire.nhs.uk/learning-disabilities-sensory-processing

Support organisations

ADDitude: www.additudemag.com

Middletown Centre for Autism: https://sensory-processing.middletownautism.com

Sensory Spectacle: www.sensoryspectacle.co.uk

CHAPTER 10: OBSESSIVE COMPULSIVE DISORDER

Further reading

Jassi, A. (2013) *Can I Tell You About OCD?* London: Jessica Kingsley Publishers.

Jassi, A. (2021) *Challenge Your OCD!* London: Jessica Kingsley Publishers.

Martin, S. and Costello, C. (2008) *The Everything Parent's Guide to Children with OCD.* Fairfield, OH: Adams Media.

Saunders, C. (2015) *Parenting OCD: Down to Earth Advice From One Parent to Another.* London: Jessica Kingsley Publishers.

Wells, J. (2021) *Touch and Go Joe: An Adolescent's Experience of OCD.* London: Jessica Kingsley Publishers.

Support organisations

Mind: www.mind.org.uk/information-support/types-of-mental-health-problems/obsessive-compulsive-disorder-ocd/about-ocd

OCD Action: www.ocdaction.org.uk

OCD UK: http://ocduk.org

OCD Youth, the site for young people with OCD: http://ocdyouth.org

Well at School, supporting young people with mental health problems: www.wellatschool.org/ocd

YoungMinds, mental health in young people: www.youngminds.org.uk

CHAPTER 11: TICS AND TOURETTE SYNDROME

Further reading

Cohen, B. (2009) *Front of the Class: How Tourettes Made me the Teacher I Never Had*. New York, NY: St Martins Griffin.

Leicester, M. (2014) *Can I Tell You about Tourette Syndrome?* London: Jessica Kingsley Publishers.

Stodd, S. (2020) *Me and My Tourettes*. Elizabeth Publications.

Van Bloss, N. (2006) *Busy Body: My Life with Tourettes Syndrome*. London: Fusion Press.

Walkup, J.T. Mink, J.W. and McNaught, K. (eds) (2012) *A Family's Guide to Tourette Syndrome*. Bloomington, IN: iUniverse.

Resources and information

NHS: www.nhs.uk/conditions/tourettes-syndrome

Support organisations

Tourettes Action: www.tourettes-action.org.uk

CHAPTER 12: ORGANISATIONAL SKILLS

References

Cambridge University Press (2015) *Cambridge Business English Dictionary*. Cambridge: Cambridge University Press.

Further reading

Branstetter, R. (2014) *The Everything Parents Guide to Children with Executive Functioning Disorder*. Avon, MA: Adams Media.

Gallager, R., Spira, E. and Rosenblatt, J. (2018) *The Organized Child*. New York, NY: Guilford Press.

Honas-Webb, L. (2020) *Six Super Skills for Executive Functioning*. Oakland, CA: New Harbinger.

Linton, S. (2022) *Executive Functioning Skills Printable Workbook*. Independently published.

Ostler, C. and Ward, F. (2012) *Advanced Study Skills* (3rd edn). Wakefield: SEN Marketing.

Patrick, A. (2020) *The Memory and Processing Guide for Neurodiverse Learners*. London: Jessica Kingsley Publishers.

Resources and information

Apps for dyslexia and learning disabilities: http://dyslexiahelp.umich.edu/tools/apps

British Dyslexia Association technology advice: https://bdanewtechnologies.wordpress.com/what-technology/apps

Cambridge Dictionaries Online: https://dictionary.cambridge.org/dictionary/english/organizational-skills

eChalk, a teaching site for teachers: www.echalk.co.uk

Mind mapping tools: www.educatorstechnology.com/2023/01/18-free-mind-mapping-tools-for-teachers.html

CHAPTER 13: EXAMS AND REVISION

Further reading

O'Brien, J. and Jones, A. (2004) *The Great Little Book of Brainpower* (2nd edn). The Great Little Book Company.

Ostler, C. and Ward, F. (2012) *Advanced Study Skills* (3rd edn). Wakefield: SEN Marketing.

Patrick, A. (2020) *The Memory and Processing Guide for Neurodiverse Learners*. London: Jessica Kingsley Publishers.

Pavey, B., Meehan, M. and Davis, S. (2013) *The Dyslexia-Friendly Teacher's Toolkit*. London: Sage Publications.

Exam access arrangement organisations

Joint Council for Qualifications: www.jcq.org.uk/exams-office/access-arrangements-and-special-consideration

Assistive technology which can be set into exam mode

Scanning pens: www.scanningpens.co.uk

TextAid assistive technology text-to-voice software: www.aventido.com/textaid

Texthelp assistive reading and writing support technology: www.texthelp.com/UK

INTERNATIONAL SUPPORT ORGANISATIONS

Australia

ADHD: www.adders.org/ausmap.htm

Australian Dyslexia Association: http://dyslexiaassociation.org.au

Autism Spectrum Australia: www.autismspectrum.org.au

Dyspraxia Foundation: www.dyspraxiaaustralia.com.au

OCD: http://au.reachout.com/obsessive-compulsive-disorder

PDA: www.autismawareness.com.au/aupdate/a-brief-history-of-pathological-demand-avoidance

DSF Dyslexia-SPELD Foundation: http://dsf.net.au/what-are-learning-disabilities

Tourette's Syndrome Association of Australia: https://tourette.org.au

Canada

ADHD: www.adders.org/canadamap.htm

Autism Canada: https://autismcanada.org

Dyslexia Canada: www.dyslexiacanada.org

Learning Disabilities Association of Ontario: www.ldao.ca

OCD Ottawa: www.ocdottawa.com

Parents Canada: www.parentscanada.com/preschool/dyscalculia

Tourette Syndrome Foundation of Canada: https://tourette.ca

New Zealand

ADHD New Zealand: www.adhd.org.nz

AnxietyNZ: https://anxiety.org.nz

Autism New Zealand: www.autismnz.org.nz

Dyslexia Foundation of New Zealand: www.dyslexiafoundation.org.nz

The Dyspraxia Support Group of New Zealand: https://dyspraxia.org.nz

Learning and Behavioural Charitable Trust New Zealand: www.lbctnz.co.nz

PDA Aotearoa New Zealand Facebook Group: www.facebook.com/groups/1716305355259190

SPELD (Specific Learning Differences): www.speld.org.nz

USA

American Dyslexia Association: www.american-dyslexia-association.com

Dyspraxia Foundation USA: www.dyspraxiausa.org

Learning Disabilities Association of America: https://ldaamerica.org

SPD Foundation: www.spdfoundation.net

STAR Institute (sensory processing): http://spdstar.org

Tourette Association of America: https://tourette.org

USAutism Association: www.usautism.org

Author biography

Diana Hudson has over 30 years' classroom science teaching experience. She has also trained to teach neurodiverse students. She has been a head of biology, head of year and a SENCO.

Diana has a PhD in Zoology but admits to struggling at school. She was diagnosed as having dyslexia a few years ago.

She is now focusing on increasing teacher and parent awareness of neurodiversity in the classroom and at home and regularly gives talks for teachers and parents.

Artist biography

Jon English is a freelance designer, illustrator and photographer based in Sussex in the UK. He enjoys a life of creativity and is never far away from an exciting project, venture or adventure. You can find out more about Jon by visiting www.moomar.co.uk

Diana and Jon have enjoyed working together on three books now. The first edition of this book, published in 2015, and *Exploring Science with Dyslexic Children and Teens,* published in 2022. They look forward to tackling future projects.

Index